"Lawyers who believe the evidence is the story don't understand the critical nature of how they open and close the case. Matlon's focus on theme, structure, and delivery hit the mark on what it takes to pull together what witnesses individually cannot accomplish. Matlon takes it from big picture goals down to the selection of words."

*Paul M. Lisnek, J.D., Ph.D.*
*Author, Legal Analyst, TV and Radio Anchor*
*National Lecturer on Trial and Litigation Skills*
*Chicago, IL*

"Ron Matlon's advice is practical and easy to apply. By reading his book and using his insight and research, you will be more credible and persuasive – a better advocate."

*Alan B. Parker, J.D.*
*Reminger Law Offices*
*Cleveland, OH*

"Ron Matlon's second edition is an essential text for the novice as well as the experienced advocate. The novice advocate will quickly benefit from Matlon's clear and practical advice. The experienced advocate will benefit from use of the end-of-chapter recommendations as a checklist to tighten up and polish current practices."

*Chris Dominic, President and Senior Consultant*
*Tsongas Litigation Consulting, Inc.*
*Past President, American Society of Trial Consultants*
*Portland, OR*

# OPENING STATEMENTS
# CLOSING ARGUMENTS

# OPENING STATEMENTS
# CLOSING ARGUMENTS

RONALD J. MATLON, Ph.D.

Litigation Consultant, Matlon and Associates
Phoenix, Maryland
and
Executive Director, American Society of Trial Consultants
Timonium, Maryland

Second Edition, 2009

Published by Dodge Consulting & Publications
e-mail: dodgeconsulting@msn.com
or: info@dodgepublications.com

Order this book at:
www.dodgepublications.com
or www.amazon.com

or call:
253-857-7716

Library of Congress Cataloging-In-Publication Data
Matlon, Ronald J., 1938-
Opening Statements/Closing Arguments, Ronald J. Matlon
Second Edition
Includes bibliographical references and index.

ISBN 10: 0-9777511-3-9
ISBN 13: 978-0-9777511-3-6
1. Trial practice – United States. 2. Forensic oratory.
3. Summation (Law)
I. Title



Printed in the United States of America by BrioPrint

# CONTENTS

## FOREWORD

During the last decade, a new set of tools has become available to lawyers preparing for trial. These tools have been fashioned from the work of academic researchers in a variety of fields over several years.

Psychologists, sociologists, and communication researchers have been studying for decades the way in which people make decisions. Those general studies led to specific research in the legal arena focused on the response of jurors to legal reasoning, courtroom procedures, presentation of evidence, witness performance, verdict forms, jury instructions, attorney performance, and the group dynamics of deliberation.

In the mid-1960's, a number of academic researchers began applying the results of general research to specific cases. They worked with attorneys on voir dire and jury selection, on opening statement and closing argument, on the effective presentation of evidence, on persuasive techniques at trial, and on witness preparation.

They also began using research techniques to gain information about specific legal cases. They conducted community surveys, trial simulations, post-verdict interviews and focus groups in order to gain information about potential juror bias and response. These case-specific research tools are now used regularly in small and large cases, in local and high-publicity cases, in single trials and serial litigation, and by target defendants with recurring exposure in specific areas. They have also become useful for attorneys in all kinds of small to medium-sized cases looking for clearer case evaluation and issue analysis, witness preparation, and jury de-selection assistance.

By 1983, a substantial number of academics had become full-time consultants to trial attorneys. In that year, these individuals formed the American Society of Trial Consultants, a growing professional organization that as of 2008 has about 500 members nationwide.

This book summarizes academic research and applies the extensive practical experience of the author as a consultant in one particular area of trial practice, opening statements and closing arguments.

Ronald J. Matlon, Ph.D.

# OPENING STATEMENTS
# CLOSING ARGUMENTS

# INTRODUCTION

To do well in court, you must be a master of communication. Specifically, your ability to perform well in trials requires that you incorporate principles of persuasion in your opening statements and closing arguments. That is what this book is about - helping you to better influence judges and juries. The book offers a trial consultant's perspective on effective opening statements and closing arguments.

And what is that perspective? I am not a lawyer. I am a communications scholar and consultant who has been studying trial advocacy for the past four decades. Essentially, I have been asking: "What persuades judges and juries in court?" What is brought to bear in this book toward answering that question are summaries of applicable research projects in communication and social psychology, advice from successful trial attorneys with years of field experience, and observations I have made while working side by side with lawyers on a variety of cases as a legal communications consultant.

To begin, view yourself as an advocate-persuader. An advocate is someone who espouses a cause through argument. Lawyers who train for courtroom battles are advocates by profession. Effective advocacy requires effective persuasion, which means leading the minds of a jury or judge to your point of view. Your task in court is to bring about attitudinal change.

As a trial lawyer, you should take two essential steps in guiding the process of attitudinal change: (1) analyze the audience; and (2) adapt to that audience. Noted attorney James Jeans writes that effective advocate-persuaders do not confine their efforts to the sterile adduction of facts:

> Every action, every word, every gesture of the attorney, his client, his witness, will filter through the mind of each juror, assume the flavor of his experience and background, blend with the distillates

> from his fellow "fact finders" and generate a feeling for the case. This then will be the concern of the advocate – to create the proper "feeling," cultivate the response mood, generate a desire to reach the "right" conclusion. In doing so, you will incidentally, but only incidentally, produce the facts that will support that desire.[1]

In other words, motivating an audience is the key to success. It is, after all, easy to dismiss the psychological and motivational dimensions of a trial, and your adversary could be gaining an important advantage over you by recognizing and utilizing these facets. One of the most consensually shared values in our legal system is the view that trial outcomes should be decided on the facts, evidence, and reasoned arguments presented by the contesting parties. This vision of the trial portrays it as a rational, rule-governed event. Juries and judges are supposed to determine what really existed or happened. Obviously, this description, which represents the ideal, does not truly reflect the social and psychological realities of what a trial actually is, namely, an exercise in persuasion.

In order for you to persuade (that is, to cause a judge-jury attitude to shift toward your position), you must involve your audience in the planning and installing of attitude change, which means emotionally stimulating their motives and needs to the point where they favor your cause. At every part of the trial, there should be an integrated effort by you to prove your case and secure that desired change. There is no recess from persuasion during a trial. It exists in jury selection, opening statements, examination of witnesses, closing arguments, judge instructions to the jury, and jury deliberations. The focus in this book, however, is strictly on opening statements and closing arguments.

PART ONE

# OPENING STATEMENTS

## THE RHETORIC OF THE OPENING STATEMENT

The trial, from beginning to end, is a rhetorical campaign. Rhetoric is the art of persuasion, and one way of thinking about the trial as a rhetorical campaign is to see it as analogous to a play with a very strong message. The author of the play is attempting to get the members of the audience to change their beliefs, attitudes, and/or behavior in response to the play's plot line. The same can be true in court. You become the playwright. Voir dire is the time when the audience reads the program and learns something about the production. The opening statement is equivalent to the first scene in a play. It is designed to capture the audience's attention. The first scene of many of Shakespeare's plays is a prologue or an introductory speech specifically designed to capture the audience's imagination. So it goes with the opening statement in court. Indeed, some lawyers, perhaps even you, consider the opening statement to be the most important part of a trial.

## THE OPENING STATEMENT: PRIMACY

Exactly how important is the opening statement? An overview of a principle called *primacy* helps us to answer that question.

### PRIMACY DEFINED

The rule of primacy is that *first impressions are lasting impressions.* What is believed first is believed intensely and is retained more vividly, and for a longer period of time. Furthermore, change regarding initial belief is resisted more forcefully.

Primacy is not to be confused with the principle of recency, which holds that the last message heard is the easiest one to remember. Primacy relates to belief and attitude formation. The side effectively presenting an issue first has an opportunity to influence beliefs and attitudes more strongly than a later presentation by the opposite side, even though both presentations may be equally potent in their impact. So if the plaintiff or prosecutor gets a jury to believe their case from the beginning, this constitutes the primacy effect at trial.

### EARLY PRIMACY RESEARCH

Most of the primacy research to date has derived from studies in which two communications of relatively equal persuasive content on a controversial issue are presented, but the order is reversed with each audience (pro/con and con/pro). In nearly all of the studies, "the nearer one comes to achieving primacy in the sense of the first presentation of unfamiliar material, the more apt one is to obtain primacy effects."[2] In other words, the first information received by members of an audience influences their impressions, beliefs, and attitudes much more intensely than the information they receive in a second (later) communication.

Primacy research began with a pioneering study done in 1925. Involved were affirmative/negative communications of equal length and persuasiveness on three controversial issues-equal political rights, the protective tariff, and monogamous marriages. Some groups (college students) heard an affirmative/negative sequence; other groups heard the reverse order. Audience attitudes were measured before and after. In all instances, there was a net attitude change in favor of the first communication presented.[3]

Two other interesting research efforts underscore the impact of first impressions on later judgments. A classic 1946 study conducted by an information theorist found that attitudes toward a hypothetical person were more positive when favorable information appeared first, and more negative when unfavorable information was presented first. In this study, subjects were given information about an imaginary individual. The information was arranged either in a favorable to unfavorable order, or vice versa. Subjects then rated the individual, and the results showed the primacy effect.[4]

A seminal study, conducted in 1957, found that once people form an initial impression, they tend not to believe subsequent information that conflicts with it. Here, two paragraphs were created that described a fictitious person, Jim, as either extroverted or introverted. Four groups of students read both paragraphs and were asked to evaluate Jim as friendly or unfriendly. When they read the "extroverted" paragraph first, they rated Jim friendly. When they read the "introverted" paragraph first, they rated him unfriendly. The first block of information was the most influential and, thus, the primacy effect was apparent.[5]

## PRIMACY IN THE COURTROOM

Does the principle of primacy apply to opening statements in the courtroom as well? Primacy was systematically studied in a trial setting for the first time in 1940. A research team questioned mock jurors and found that some of them formed and held strong opinions after opening statements. Evidence presented later was viewed in the context of what was said by counsel during the opening.[6] In other words, opening statements formed the structure for later judgments; first impressions created lasting impressions. Later research on primacy in the courtroom dealt with the order in which opening statements are presented. Does the right to speak first give that attorney an advantage over his or her opponent?[7] One researcher uncovered a primacy effect when two-thirds of the mock jurors in this study (1969) reached a verdict consistent with the first opening statement presented, regardless of which side delivered their opening statement first. (Half of the subjects heard the prosecution first and half heard the defense.)[8]

A strong opening statement from a prosecutor or plaintiff's counsel can often make a major difference in trials. Researchers at the University of Kansas investigated the effects of both in-depth and abbreviated opening statements on jurors' verdicts. Some opening remarks used in the research contained very brief (abbreviated) preview conditions; other opening remarks were more extensive (in-depth). The mock criminal trial in this study dealt with transporting stolen goods across state lines. The study (1981) found that jurors were heavily influenced by whatever in-depth or extensive opening they heard first. If the prosecution's opening was extensive, the defendant was found guilty regardless of the extensiveness of the defense's opening statement. If the prosecution's opening was abbreviated and the defense made extensive remarks, the verdict in the same case was not guilty.[9]

In much of the research, the phenomenon of primacy was found to occur because the first speech received more attention than the second speech;[10] the first speech had less interference for the audience than the second speech;[11] and the first speech had the advantage of structuring the context and interpreting what happened for the audience.[12] Put another way, interesting subject matter, controversial topics, and highly familiar stories tend toward primacy.[13] Attention and receptivity levels of your audience are usually highest during the opening minutes of any communication. Hence, what you say first may shape the way your audience perceives and learns everything that follows.[14] This may well mean that if a case is inherently dramatic, interesting and not too technical (such as an emotionally contested divorce, a savage murder, or a rape), it will allow the primacy effect to occur. That party will secure audience belief first, giving the party a distinct advantage. All of this information clearly emphasizes the significance of three communication considerations discussed later in this book: attention factors, two-sided presentations, and the development of a case theme using narrative language.

Primacy in litigation may not be absolute because courtroom conditions differ from those in most primacy experiments. As one researcher notes, primacy is not "an indubitable factor in persuasion," but occurs only on certain occasions.[15] One condition that may detract from the primacy advantage to the prosecutor or plaintiff occurs when the jury is given case-specific information during voir dire.[16] Furthermore, the prosecution and plaintiff have a burden of proof different from the burden found in non-legal disputes. So it is not exactly known to what degree the principle of primacy can be extrapolated to the courtroom setting.[17] No one can quantify with precision how significant opening statements are in litigation. We at least know that they are of such value that the plaintiff's attorney or prosecutor should prepare and present an opening statement that is extremely persuasive to the jury. Just as a coach uses strategy in a football game, you should try to get your game out of reach through the opening statement, and have the other side play catch-up for the rest of the trial.

But what about the defense attorney? How should he or she adapt to the primacy phenomenon? Should the defense wait to present opening statements until after the plaintiff or prosecution have called all of their witnesses?

There are both advantages and disadvantages in attorneys reserving opening statements. Advantages are: (1) a delayed opening buys time to allow for flexibility in theme development for the defense, and (2) it hides information and strategies from opposing counsel until later in the trial. The first seems more valid than the second, since pretrial conferences and discovery make the surprise element in the opening statement highly unlikely.

The disadvantages are: (1) the jury may infer that the defense position is so weak that no opening statement is possible, and (2) as mentioned, the primacy advantage held by a prosecutor or plaintiff speaking first is not diminished by any rebuttal by defendants. The following illustrates the importance to the defense of positioning the opening statement.

> A killing occurred a few years back in my county on a dance floor with roughly fifty people present. The single eyewitness of the shooting was named Lucy and the victim was her father-in-law (with whom she was living at the time, and the two were a couple at the dance lounge that night.) With some vigor and intensity, the defense gave an early opening statement focusing primarily on Lucy's character, especially the fact that she was living with her father-in-law. Although such habitation circumstances may not seem shocking to the reader, there are still people in rural Colorado who find them so. In any event, during the speech, the defense did a pretty good impeachment job on the state's single eyewitness, Lucy. As she walked through the courtroom to take her seat in the witness box, the jury gave her a long and cold small-town stare. She had been fatally contaminated by the defense. Of course, the defense could have waited and could have hurt her during cross-examination, but she would have testified for an hour under direct testimony, as a pristine bereaved lady, and the impact would have probably made a lasting impression on the jury. But because the defense made the proper choice of offering the opening statement early, the direct testimony of Lucy was viewed with suspicion at best. The jury, then, saw and heard a different state case than had the opening statement been held for later presentation. The defense had ground the glasses for the jury and had influenced what they saw.[18]

# THE OPENING STATEMENT: DEVELOPING A THEME

After opening statements, a case unfolds, not necessarily in any organized manner, but in bits and pieces. The opening statement is your best opportunity to put your entire message in a compact package so that the jury and/or judge will be able to get a bird's eye view that allows them to better comprehend and appreciate the issues and the evidence. The opening statement is a preview, road map, or synopsis of what is to follow. Its place in the trial follows the old bromide for public speakers: "Tell them what you're going to tell them (opening statement), tell them (evidence), and then tell them what you told them (closing argument)."

## RATIONALE FOR DEVELOPING A THEME

In order to facilitate the processing of information, the opening statement must provide a single theme or a small number of themes that jurors and the judge can use to integrate witness testimony. Too many themes (or too many defenses) bog a case down and confuse the audience. Hence, thematic development should be kept simple. A thematic framework may be defined as "a subset of existing knowledge, based on prior experience and relevant to a limited domain, that people use as a framework to guide their observation, organization, and retrieval from memory of perceived events."[19] These frameworks help jurors make sense out of a rather disjointed array of information that comes forward in a trial. Thus, themes help jurors filter information by placing focus on what you intend to emphasize in your case.

In addition, themes facilitate juror and judge recall of important aspects of your case.[20] They affect memory by determining what will be attended to. They are encoded in memory and act as an anchor for organizing new information, and guiding later retrieval of that information.[21]

Human understanding and accurate recall of facts are enhanced by the use of themes. One cognitive psychologist maintains that we understand and remember characters best when we can identify with their goals.[22] Some experimental work in cognition illustrates that as people enhance their understanding of a character's goals, motives, and plans, that character's actions are more easily recalled.[23] One researcher gave his subjects a story about a farmer who tried to put his donkey into its shed. Some of the subjects read a paragraph with this goal explicitly stated. Others read a themeless paragraph without the ultimate goal mentioned. When the ultimate goal was omitted, subjects found the text only half as comprehensible, and they remembered 20 percent fewer action items than the first group. Thus, *stories with stated themes help audiences more effectively integrate information.* Themes determine what audiences pay attention to and what they encode into memory. Themes act as frameworks for organizing information. Finally, themes guide the retrieval of information from memory. Without knowing personal goals, motives, and plans of witnesses called to the stand, jurors have difficulty accurately recalling and understanding those witnesses' actions. In fact, social science research indicates that trial verdicts tend to favor the party who creates a thematic framework in the opening statement over those who do not develop themes.[24]

## LOCATING THE RIGHT THEME

How do you find an appropriate theme or themes? A nationally-recognized trial consultant proposes that an effective theme should be holistic, economical, memorable, and easy to use.[25] A holistic theme addresses your case comprehensively by focusing on one issue (e.g., damages). An economical theme uses the fewest possible words (e.g., taking responsibility). A memorable theme might include such devices as alliteration, metaphor, familiarity, or a catchy phrase (e.g., "Where's the beef?"). More will be said later about thematic language. Finally, an easy to use theme is one that is simple to say and repeat throughout the trial (e.g., "It's just a red herring.").

Basically, the facts of the case point toward themes. As you continue to gather facts, you should think of the possible themes that surround those facts. Jeans offers the following illustration of an attorney's theme development based on facts:

> Plaintiff is injured when struck by a blade which disengages from a rotary lawn mower operated by A and owned by B. A is college student who earns money during the summer cutting grass. He has operated many lawn mowers, is an engineering student, and is familiar with their mechanics. He has worked for B on other occasions, was familiar with B's lawn mower. On a previous occasion he had noticed that the blade was wobbly and had notified B. In fact, B had owned the lawn mower for four years and had never had it repaired or overhauled. B acknowledges that A had told him that the blade was wobbly. Assume your suit is against A alone. Your opening statement will attempt to exonerate B from any wrongdoing and lay the blame on A's feet. The theme to be developed will be as follows:
>
> A is trained and experienced with lawn mowers. He discovered that the lawn mower was faulty but continued to use it knowing and appreciating the risks that were involved. B, on the other hand, had reason to believe the lawn mower was in working order. It had functioned properly for four years without the need of repair. He was told by A that the blade was wobbly but he didn't think that this was a dangerous situation. He knew that A was an engineering student, well versed in the handling of lawn mowers, and relied on him to make any necessary repairs or at least tell B that the mower was dangerous and needed repair.
>
> If the suit were against B alone, the theme would be substantially different and proceed as follows:
>
> B had owned the lawn mower for four years and during the entire 48 months had not attended to its servicing or repair. He had been told specifically that the blade was wobbly. But rather than have

> the blade replaced at minimal cost, he elected to expose A and others to the dangers of a malfunctioning power lawn mower. A, a hardworking and conscientious college student, having told B of the defect, assumed that the simple repair had been made.[26]

The facts are the same, only the slant has changed. Once you determine the theme or thread woven through the case, you then *embed it in the minds of the judge and jury in the opening statement, emphasize it throughout the questioning of witnesses, and stress it once again in summation.*

But once again, you are reminded to keep the theme simple. It will be easier for the jury to remember, and if successful, the jurors will use the language of your theme in deliberations. For example, in a medical malpractice case against a doctor and a hospital, the plaintiff's theme might be "Just a simple X-ray was all that was needed." Or in a priest sexual abuse case against a Roman Catholic diocese, the defense theme might be "We all believed that the power of prayer would solve the problem." In these two examples, we want the jurors to use the words "simple X-ray" and "power of prayer" during their deliberations.

One successful trial advocate has identified four representative themes that can be used in opening statements:[27]

1. The *underdog theme,* which might be developed by a plaintiff suing a giant corporation. The underdog is a little person trying to fight city hall, David up against Goliath, a person with whom many jurors can empathize. Recall all the underdog boxers who managed to get the spectators to cheer them on.
2. The *undefeated theme,* which focuses on the indomitable fighter who never quits, regardless of the odds. Ernest Hemingway's favorite bullfighter, Monolete, and the old fisherman in *The Old Man and the Sea* are classic examples of the person who never succumbs to defeat. If you point out that the disfigured and paralyzed plaintiff bravely continues to function and fight, the jury may find that person truly heroic.

3. The *victim theme*, which deals with people who are put upon by everyone. Charlie Chaplin's characters were victims of society and progress. In the film *Modern Times,* Chaplin was actually sucked into the gears of a machine and spit out the other end. The plaintiff in a consumer fraud case can be portrayed as a victim of advertising, and jurors may become outraged at the defendant. Or if there has been a permanent disfigurement as the result of an unsafe consumer product, the victim's attorney may focus on the theme of a "lifetime lawsuit." Even the defense can develop a victim theme in a case built on self-defense.
4. The *contrasts theme* creates startling images for the jury. Simple contrasts that few jurors can miss are the best: small-big, weak-strong, human-impersonal, simple-complex, moral-immoral, or careful-careless. In a child dart-out case, think of what can be done by contrasting a 40-pound little girl with 2½ ton truck. Or again, the little guy versus the huge corporation.

Themes are powerful concepts; they require no exaggeration on your part because they are so deeply rooted in our belief-attitude-value structure. You need to search for effective themes as you think about preparing and presenting your opening statement.

### RECOMMENDATIONS FOR DEVELOPING A THEME

- Select only one or a very few pertinent themes
- Keep the theme simple
- Build the theme around the most salient case facts
- Common themes refer to underdogs, undefeated, victims, and contrasts
- Repeat your theme during voir dire, the opening statement, witness examination, and closing arguments

## THE OPENING STATEMENT: CONTENT AND STRUCTURE

As in any good speech, the opening statement has an introduction, a body, and a conclusion. We will begin our discussion of content and structure by reviewing remarks and examples offered by prosecutors and plaintiff attorneys.

### PLAINTIFF OR PROSECUTION OPENING STATEMENT

The purpose of the opening statement should be explained in the *introduction*. Here is an example: "This is my first opportunity to talk to you about this case. It is not my intention to persuade you to my point of view or to argue a specific point of the facts. This speech serves as a skeleton or framework upon which you can place the testimony as it unfolds at the trial. I believe that with this framework you will better be able to grasp the issues involved."[28] Next, the order of the trial should be noted, if this has not already been done by the judge.

As part of the introduction, you should identify the key people involved in the lawsuit. Describe *who* they are. These key individuals might be asked by you to stand for all the jury to see. This might include your client, others on the trial team, and any critical witnesses who possibly might be present. The jury is not familiar with the people in your case, so you need to show them a "program," especially if there are many key characters. A photo and/or name chart, along with the role each person plays, can also be helpful to your audience.

Each introduction should be designed to humanize your parties so that the jury and judge can relate to them as real persons. For instance, plaintiff's attorney might say: "Catherine Doyle is a high school teacher. Before October of this year, she was a very healthy young woman, 31 years of age. Catherine is married and the mother of one 5-year-old son, Martin. She enjoyed jogging, bicycling, and tennis. Never during the course of any of these activities did she ever have trouble with her leg." These standard introductory routines, combined with elements to spark the jury's attention, prime the judge and jury to listen to what follows. Even when your client is a corporation, it needs to be humanized. One way to do this is to show photographs of the corporate officials involved in the case if they are not present.

After you introduce your audience to *who* is involved, you then need to guide their attention to *what* happened, *where* it happened, *when* it happened, and why it happened. For instance, in a personal injury case, you may want to raise the following questions: What did the defendant do that was wrong? Where did this incident occur? When did it take place? Why did it happen? What is your own theory of the case? What happened to the plaintiff? What is the nature of the plaintiff's injuries? How severe are they? All of these questions should be answered in capsule form early in your opening statement. Here is an illustration from an automobile rear-end collision case:

> Ladies and gentlemen, this lawsuit was filed because the defendant's car was following too closely behind the car of Catherine Doyle, the plaintiff. The two cars were driving westbound on Allegheny Avenue on June 20 of last year. The defendant, Mr. Powers, was not paying attention to the traffic ahead of him. As a result, Catherine was hit from behind by Mr. Powers. She suffered a broken and separated leg, and she will have this injury for the rest of her life.[29]

Note that not everything that will develop in the case is here. Important material has been separated from the unimportant. The best trial lawyers follow the practice of narrowing the story as much as possible during the opening statement. Virtually all the experts agree that simplicity should be your goal. Most jurors lose interest if the task before them seems too complicated. In fact, you should tell the jury their task is a relatively simple one. This remark is rhetorically compelling because it reduces jurors' anxiety over their perceived burden of deciding complex issues.

You have now, in your introduction, given your audience the well-known "five W's" of the journalist. You have presented to them in broad strokes the who, what, where, when and why of the case. In doing so, you have immediately set up a story line for your case, stimulated your audience's interest, and fostered their comprehension.

The *body* of the opening statement contains the bulk of the necessary information, which should virtually never be presented indifferently. If the information imparted in the body is kept general, the audience may well see you as being uninterested in what you are saying, unprepared, and uncommitted to your position. Detail must be provided. Counsel should not merely claim that Catherine Doyle was driving carefully, but should succinctly state the facts supporting that claim. It is, of course, easy to go overboard with detailing. The shotgun approach regarding details should be strictly avoided. Presenting pertinent detail is essential; presenting every single detail is poor strategy. In other words, the body of the opening statement provides you with the opportunity to become a master storyteller. "This does not mean that storytelling in trials subverts justice. Rather, it points out that most social conflicts... are so complex, it is impossible or impractical to present detailed descriptions of them in a courtroom. Lawyers must simplify and organize the event so jurors can understand it. Storytelling has accomplished this goal for years."[30]

Storytelling becomes the "everyday form of communication that enables a diverse cast of courtroom characters to follow the development of a case and reason about the issues in it."[31] The story is the underlying judgment scheme by which different people communicate with each other about issues and evidence in legal cases. Through storytelling techniques, you can present issues and evidence in a way that allows a jury to transform the issues and evidence into a meaningful story. "Stories are systematic means of storing, bringing up to date, rearranging, comparing, testing, and interpreting available information about social behavior."[32] You must help your audience in court to reconstruct events and actions through effective storytelling. Stories allow audiences to coherently structure an event or action in much the same way that they unravel mystery novels, movies, news stories, or television situation comedies.

What does a storytelling approach to the body of the opening of the statement entail? As in any good story, plot, timeframes, characters, setting, motive, and action are essential. In the civil case regarding Catherine Doyle, the attorneys should focus on scene, liability, injury, and, if permitted, damages. However, within that structure, a chronological sequence of events should unfold. Audiences prefer a story that has a beginning, a middle, and an end. The opening statement should not deviate from that simple pattern. Let's follow a personal injury case to show how a story can unfold in chronological order.

In many civil personal injury cases, *scene* is important. Start the scene on a positive note. Talk about Catherine's happy and productive day before she got into the car. Tell us where she is going. Lead us slowly to where and when the incident took place and what happened. For instance, the scene where Mr. Powers hit Catherine Doyle from behind should be described meticulously. Details of that occurrence will be important to jurors. Description of the vehicles, date and time, weather conditions, road conditions, and actions that took place are likely to be very relevant in the jurors' minds.

Of course, if the alleged cause of the accident is not another driver, but an automotive manufacturer's design defect, then the story starts somewhere else. The scene in that story is the office of the automaker who years earlier made the decision to put profits over people.

As the story of what happened comes to an end, the question of why it took place should be addressed. It is at this point that the plaintiff's attorney assigns *liability* to the defendant. In fact, this point ought to be a motivational peak in the counsel's speech. Here, legal concepts should be discussed only in general terms. It is more important to show via emotion why the defendant is to blame.[33]

The discussion of *injury* should include a vivid account of the harm done. However, it is crucial that the judge and jury understand the medical jargon. You can begin talking about injury by clearly describing (1) the anatomy of the injured area or organ (in both lay and medical terms), and (2) the method of treatment required (in both lay and technical terminology). For example:

> Doctor Harris had to perform surgery on Catherine's leg, and you will hear him tell you about that surgery. The operation is called an open reduction of the tibia and fibula. Briefly, what Dr. Harris did was to cut open the lower part of her leg so he could see and handle the two lower leg bones that had been broken and separated in the accident. Then, with his hands, he actually moved the bones back together in their normal position. To hold these broken pieces together while the bones healed, he then drilled holes in the bones with an electric drill so that screws could be placed into Catherine's bones, locking them together.

After this description, you can go into the prognosis, medication, and therapy for Catherine Doyle. Medical experts who will testify about her situation can be introduced.

Many states do not allow counsel to mention the amount of compensation in a civil lawsuit. In other jurisdictions, recoverable damages or legal losses can be discussed in the opening statement of a civil case. You must be cautious here not to exaggerate, and you must remain calm and somber. In other words, you should not claim more for the client than can reasonably be expected from the jury. When you plead for relief in an opening statement, it is not prudent to "overkill" with data. Doing so may cause a jury to become anxious and overwhelmed. Bombarding the jurors with huge amounts of data may make them feel the case is not really as simple as it perhaps had seemed.

Regardless of dollar figures, you must explain how the evidence will illustrate each category of loss. How much should be recovered for out-of-pocket expenses? Loss of earnings? Pain and suffering? Mental anguish? Inability to lead a normal life? The University of Chicago studies on jury deliberation conclude with an interesting finding: "A case involving several items of damage was submitted to numerous juries in two different ways. On the one hand, a separate verdict was rendered by the jury on each item of damage, while on the other hand, a lump sum verdict was returned. Where separate verdicts were returned on each of the items of damage, they totaled a higher amount than where a lump sum verdict was returned. This would indicate that it is the duty of the attorney, in states where the use of per diem formulas is allowed, to use them in cases where separate items of damage exist."[34]

While itemizing damages is essential for the plaintiff, social psychology research has shown that jurors give money for "worthwhile purposes."[35] Plaintiffs must show they have hope for the future, and the jury should know from the beginning of trial about that hope and how the money is to be used. Many jurors keep damages on the low side by claiming that the money will not ease the pain or bring back the dead. So it is to your benefit, as the plaintiff's attorney, to let the jurors know that your client wants to work again or to help others in his or her family. Jurors are more likely to "fix and help" than to "compensate and award."

Once damages have been discussed, your story is now over. The actual end of the story is, of course, in the hands of the jury and/or judge, and you should tell them so. (See the section "Language and Style" for additional tips on storytelling.)

In a graceful and succinct conclusion of an opening statement, the prosecutor or plaintiff's counsel should recap the highlights of the case, the issues to be considered, and the theme or theory to be developed. These closing words should be upbeat. In other words, you should display confidence that your case will prevail.

The conclusion should also contain an explicit, not an implicit, appeal. The jury or judge should not have to infer what the attorney wants; they should be instructed specifically about what they should feel, believe, and do. Explicit appeals are by far the more persuasive for the plaintiff and prosecution. For example, you might close your opening statement with these remarks: "At the end of the trial, you will go to the jury room to search for the truth. When you return, I know that you will hold your heads up high and justice will be done when you say, "The defendant is solely to blame for Catherine's injuries." This appeal is much more explicit than asking for the jury to "do what is right." Although you are forbidden from revealing your own personal feelings about the case, this ban does not preclude you from directly stating to a jury what decision(s) they should reach. Telling them explicitly what their decision should be is an excellent technique of persuasion.[36] (See the section for plaintiff/prosecutor in the box, "Recommendations for the Content and Structure of Opening Statements.")

## DEFENSE COUNSEL OPENING STATEMENT

The opening statement for the defense essentially follows the same basic pattern: retelling the same story but with different emphases and/or a different set of developing themes. For example, the attorney for Mr. Powers might express regret that Ms. Doyle was injured, but indicate that the accident was her fault, or that no one can be blamed for what happened because it was truly accidental.

It is also critical that the defense lawyer, during an opening statement, establish a sense of identification between the defendant and the jury. A common bond of sympathy should be found and exploited. For instance, the plaintiff's attorney may say in a negligence case that it was the ice and snow on Mr. Smith's sidewalk that caused the plaintiff to slip and fall. In reply, the defense attorney, who recognizes that most of the jurors are property owners who have endeavored to keep their own sidewalks clean in the winter, might say that Mr. Smith did everything a prudent person could do to keep the sidewalk as free of ice as possible. Adapting to your audience is essential.

Also, it is best not to disclose damaging evidence that can catch the opposing prosecutor or plaintiff's attorney by surprise. Such evidence will have greater impact on the jury if it is introduced into the case by your own witnesses. Commenting on such evidence too early merely softens the impact when it is later presented by your witnesses.[37] Finally, in the conclusion to the speech, the defense lawyer should remind the jury members of their duty to keep open minds. (See the section for the defense in the box, "Recommendations for the Content and Structure of Opening Statements.")

## ADDITIONAL CONSIDERATIONS FOR ATTORNEYS FOR BOTH SIDES OF THE CASE

Now let's look at some additional matters both sides should consider in thinking through the substance of an opening statement. One consideration is *whether or not to disclose case weaknesses.* There is obviously no point in volunteering information that might damage your case if counsel for the other side does not intend to raise the weakness at trial. However, if the weakness is likely to be raised as an issue, it is wise not to try to sweep the information under the rug. You should mention the weakness, but diminish it. If, for example, a defendant in a personal injury case had been smoking marijuana, it is best to refer to this activity nonchalantly as the facts are being reconstructed. Such casual mentioning takes the sting out of the weakness right away. Opening statements provide you with an opportunity to talk frankly with a jury, and any manifestation of fairness you exhibit adds to your effectiveness.[38] Being perceived as fair helps you to establish rapport and build confidence with the jury.

You should always *take notes on the content of your opponent's opening statement.* You can use your notes to check on the other side's promises when closing arguments are given. In your own closing argument, you can point out any promises made but not kept by opposing counsel. However, during your opening statement, the opposition's case should neither be summarized nor refuted in great detail. If you discuss the opposing case at length, you run the risk of making that case appear more formidable than it really is.

This is by no means intended to infer that the opposition's case should be entirely ignored. At times, you may choose to *generally and subtly forewarn the jury or judge to watch for certain expected weak information in the opposition's case.* Psychological research shows that individuals resist counterinfluence to a greater degree when they have been forewarned by prior exposure to the arguments involved.[39] This principle is analogous to that of being inoculated against a disease. But here, jurors are learning to inoculate themselves against persuasive appeals from the counterarguments. The mechanism here seems to be that when individuals are forewarned of a pending persuasion attempt, they immediately begin to generate counterarguments to what they anticipate hearing.[40]

This point was illuminated by social psychologists in the following experiment. One group of college students was told that they would be hearing a lecture from a campus housing director advocating that all freshmen and sophomores be required to live in dormitories. Another group, which was not forewarned about the speaker, was asked to write out their thoughts on the issue. A third group was told nothing. All three groups then heard the same lecture. Those who were forewarned (inoculated) about the persuasion attempt and those who were asked to think and write about the topic resisted the position of the lecturer to a much greater degree than those who received no prior instructions at all.[41] These findings indicate that forewarning induces resistance, which is particularly useful information for plaintiffs and prosecutors to know.

Asking the jury or judge to compare the strength of your own arguments to the weaknesses in the opposition's arguments (called "two-sided" presentations) is a highly effective strategy with better-educated juries.[42] *At least some attempt should be made with an educated jury to create a two-sided approach in the opening statement* in order to engage jurors on a cognitive level as analyst-participants in the trial. In contrast, two-sided presentations should be avoided with jurors who tend to view matters emotionally. Such people are looking to be guided in a different way. They do not respond well to long, tedious, step-by-step accounts, which are too complex for them to absorb. Rather, they most appreciate it when you provide them with three or four critical points upon which to base their verdicts.[43] Identifying which jurors tend toward the rational and which to the emotional is a matter of individual experience and perception, as is the decision on which approach to take regarding two-sided presentations when the jury is a mixture of these attributes.

Another consideration in designing an opening statement concerns how much to claim. The best advice to follow is not to open a door so wide that it cannot be closed. You should *never go further than your proof will allow.* To do so can be disastrous, since jurors or opposing counsel inevitably recall the overstated representation. The failure to live up to a promise can make your case appear far weaker than it really is. One interesting study found that opening statements that exaggerated the strength of prosecutorial evidence resulted in more lenient verdicts than opening statements that avoided overstated promises. However, this effect is nullified when the defense *points out* the exaggeration during its summation.[44] Furthermore, deliberately including matters that cannot be established by admissible evidence may constitute a fatal error for you.[45] For instance, mistrial can be declared if a criminal prosecutor makes a remark such as, "I suspect the defendant has done things far worse than we can prove. He really is a rotten guy!"

Following common law, *the opening statement must not be perceived as argument.* Argument or persuasion is technically to be saved until all the evidence is in and summations are offered to the jury. In other words, you are prevented "from encouraging inferences or conclusions from abstracted data until the abstracted data has been actually adduced in the trial event."[46] Here is an illustration of argument in the opening statement that would probably be ruled out of order. An attorney says, "The defendant, Mr. Powers, negligently drove at an excessive rate of speed." This phrasing constitutes argument because it is up to the jury to decide if Powers was negligent. Counsel cannot draw that conclusion, nor can Mr. Powers himself, nor can any of the witnesses.

This rule against argument does not mean that opening statements have to be lukewarm and sterile. Quite the contrary. You can still say, "The speedometer read 73 mph and Mr. Powers was driving in a 50 mph zone." You may even be able to say that "Mr. Powers was racing down the road at 73 mph!" All this can be voiced because there will be witnesses who will appear on the stand to state these facts to the court. But, the conclusion of negligence cannot be uttered or inferred in the opening statement because it constitutes argument.

How does one determine where to draw the line? Judges differ radically in interpreting what constitutes impermissible argument.[47] Can the jury make such fine distinctions? Probably not. After all, there are many ways that you may persuade without arguing; the distinction is subtle.[48] Does the rule that attorneys can be persuasive only in closing arguments ignore clear reality? Many legal communication experts believe it does. One states, "Communication theorists... now accept the broad concept that being persuaded relates to three behavioral outcomes: attitude formation, attitude reinforcement, and attitude change. What we call 'informative communication' serves a persuasive function in that it conditions jurors to respond in a certain way. Attitude formation begins at the point where the jurors receive their first piece of information and intensifies as more information is received."[49] This passage certainly describes a typical opening statement.

One final consideration about opening statements regards the use of objections. As a rule of thumb, *one should use objections sparingly during opening statements.* Objections might be used if opposing counsel makes an inference but presents it as fact, if issues of law are being analyzed, or if certain facts declared inadmissible in pretrial motions are alluded to in the presentation by counsel for the other side. You should raise an objection only if you are reasonably certain that the judge will sustain it. After all, you can create an initially poor impression if your objections are constantly being overruled while the other side is speaking. The jury may regard this interruption during opening statement as an attempt by you to confuse the opponent and break the line of thought. Also consider that a restrained delivery deters objections from the other side better than a forceful delivery.[50]

If you should wish to avoid objections to the content of your opening statement, omit objectionable material of the kind just noted. However, if an objection is raised against you, you should dispassionately present your side of the argument only if the judge requests it and you desire to do so. If the judge interrupts your opening statement with a question, as is commonly the case in bench trials, you should answer it and then go on with your opening at the point where you left off.

## RECOMMENDATIONS FOR THE CONTENT AND STRUCTURE OF OPENING STATEMENTS

### FOR THE PLAINTIFF/PROSECUTOR

- State the purpose of the opening statement
- Explain the order of the trial
- Identify key characters; humanize your own characters
- Explain what happened, where it happened, and how it happened in capsule form
- Tell the entire story in some detail; organize the story chronologically. (For example, in a personal injury case, vividly describe the scene, clearly explain liability, graphically describe the injury, and, if possible, outline damages.)
- Restate the theme, the highlights of the case, and the issues to be proven
- Appeal explicitly to the jury for a decision in your favor

### FOR THE DEFENSE

- Retell the story in chronological order, but with a different emphasis and theme
- Find and develop a bond between the defendant and the jury
- Withhold references to damaging evidence that might surprise your opponent
- Remind the jurors to keep an open mind throughout the trial

### FOR ATTORNEYS ON BOTH SIDES OF THE CASE

- Mention case weaknesses and diminish their importance
- Take notes during your opponent's opening statement; use these notes when you prepare your closing argument
- Forewarn the judge or jury to watch for evidence gaps in your opponent's case (especially with better-educated juries)
- Avoid exaggerated claims
- Avoid argument
- Use objections sparingly during opening statements

## THE OPENING STATEMENT: PRESENTATION

Like any public speech worth its salt, the opening statement must utilize certain presentational techniques that enhance its persuasive potential. Three such techniques will be reviewed here: language and style, attention factors, and delivery.

### LANGUAGE AND STYLE

Good storytelling is the essence of effective narrative style. In analyzing nearly one hundred trials, a linguistic expert found that the story is a very powerful organizing device. Even when a time sequence is not followed, jurors will try to rearrange the information into a narrative storytelling form.[51] The opening statement is basically a story, and the techniques you should employ are those of the traditional storyteller. This approach is in stark contrast to presenting a review of what each witness, one by one, will say in the trial. The format for summarizing events is based on these factors:

- Establishing time and place
- Introducing the protagonist or central character around whom the action revolves
- Acquainting the audience with the problem
- Developing the plot chronologically
- Forming an ultimate, presumably happy, ending

If this format is meticulously thought through and presented, your story can hover over all the rest of the trial as the genuine gauge of reality against which the jury measures the evidence. If presented well, the story can almost serve as an additional, influential juror during deliberations.[52]

## WORD CHOICE: STRATEGY

To make narration effective, certain strategic word choices must be used. A communication educator who investigated the use of attorney language in criminal trials discovered a couple of interesting things: first, that successful prosecutors are verbally assertive and direct, whereas unsuccessful prosecutors are polite and hesitant; second, that prosecutors should avoid words such as *please, I hope, I think,* and *maybe* in favor of words such as *very* and *certain*.[53] This researcher found successful defense lawyers to be abstract and ambiguous, and unsuccessful defense attorneys to be clear and specific. For example, heavy use of adverbs makes a difference to the prosecutor inasmuch as they increase specificity. This makes sense because it is the prosecutor who must clearly fulfill the burden of proof, while the defense need only create doubt.

The powerful principle of primacy was discussed earlier. That principle applies to word choice strategy as well. The first words to come out of your mouth in an opening statement must be powerful ones. Here is an example of a typical opening: "Ladies and Gentlemen of the jury, I thank you for being here today. Your duty to serve as a juror is an important one, and my client and I trust that you will execute that duty with . . . ." At best, such openings are not memorable; at worst they are dull and unimpressive. Contrast that opening with the following: "The insurance industry faces a crisis today. If every delay in resolving claims results in a jury finding bad faith and awarding punitive damages, insurance companies will have to raise consumer premiums." The latter example started with a strong belief the attorney wanted his jury to hold during the trial and deliberations. This is the primacy effect in action.

### WORD CHOICE: IMPORTANCE

The importance of word choice in narrative style cannot be overemphasized. Consider the following:

1. Prosecutors should not refer to *the state;* such a reference is too cold and official. Rather, a prosecutor ought to refer to *the people* or, with pride, to the United States of America being against the defendant. And whom do the people represent? Naturally, they represent *the victim!* You should always use language that personalizes your side and depersonalizes your opposition. In the earlier-described hypothetical civil case *Doyle v. Powers,* the defense lawyer should refer to Doyle as the *plaintiff* and to his or her client as *Jim Powers.* The client's name should be used whenever possible.
2. Phrases such as *the evidence will show that...* or *we expect to prove beyond a reasonable doubt that...* disrupt the flow of the story and should be avoided. This language is particularly weak for prosecutors and plaintiffs because it lacks force. The phrase "we believe the evidence will show that...," if used at all, should be said only near the beginning of the opening statement and in a generic sense. You should then proceed directly to the facts and say, "The defendant, driving east on Main Street, sped right through the red light, never slowed down, and crashed right into the side of Tim King's car."
3. Some words are more appropriate for one side than they are for the other. To the plaintiff, an action was *wrong*; to the defendant, the same action was *unavoidable.* Plaintiff's counsel should refer to a *collision, crash, wreck,* or *tragedy;* defense counsel might talk about an *accident, fender-bender, mishap, or act of God.* If an automobile accident involves an injured child, the plaintiff's lawyer calls the youngster

a *playing child,* whereas the defendant's lawyer refers to the *darting child.* When referring to damages, the plaintiff should ask for *compensation to correct the wrongdoing,* while the defense attorney should not want the plaintiff to *win an award.* Appropriate language needs to be carefully selected for each case and side.

4. Technical, medical, and legal terms have to be explained in lay language in order to bridge the gap between the jury's understanding and the vocabulary of both you and your witnesses. Lacerations, abrasions, contusions, and closed fractures must be noted in terms of cuts, sprains, or broken bones. Legalese (dead legal phrases) should be avoided. *I represent the executrix of Samuel Diamond* ought to be replaced by: *In this case, I am here representing the widow of Samuel Diamond.* If legal language must be used, it should be carefully defined in lay terms. After all, technical, medical, and legal terms are mind stoppers; they communicate little.
5. Simple words should replace complex ones. In a National Science Foundation study, only one out of 35 prospective jurors understood what a *proximate cause* was after they were told that "it is a cause which, in natural and continuous sequence, produces an injury. Without proximate cause, the injury would not have occurred." Many people confused the word *proximate* with *approximate.* The only juror who understood what it meant was a Ph.D.[54] There are many words and phrases where simplicity helps. *Before* is better than *prior,* and *after* is better than *subsequent. Crossed the highway* is better than *traversed the highway. Asked the doctor* is better than *interrogated the physician. Began the operation* is better than *commenced the surgery. Get out of the truck* is better than *alight from the motor vehicle.* Verbal obfuscation should absolutely be avoided in oral presentations to juries. What you say must be understood clearly by the least-educated person in the jury box.

6. Simple sentence structure should replace complex structure. This approach, too, enhances clarity. Using simple sentences does not mean being antiseptic and uninteresting; it means being crisp and cogent.
7. Use the present tense. This actively connects your story to the jury. Story-telling is generally more engaging and persuasive when the past tense is avoided and the present tense is used.

## WORD CHOICE: IMAGERY

To transform the ordinary into the exciting, you should also incorporate imagery into your opening statement. Imagery involves creating pictures that appeal to one's senses. The ideal situation would be to present a film reenactment of the story told in the opening statement. But you obviously cannot use this technique and must therefore resort to words to make the story live. Words should make the image extremely vivid, not hazy. A vivid image is one that appeals to all the senses- sight, hearing, touch, taste, smell, muscular or kinesthetic feeling, and internal or organic sensations.

As you prepare your opening statement, think about the scenes and places in your story. "Close your eyes and focus. Listen to sounds. Become aware of scents and odors. Notice flavors and textures. The more you become aware of the client's life, .. [you will be] better able to bring their story to life."[55]

Your judge and jury should almost be able to see, hear, and/or feel directly certain elements of your case. Here are some sentences using words that appeal to three of the senses often evoked in the courtroom:

**VISUAL IMAGERY** The injured plaintiff's forehead was *split open* by the rearview mirror. His arm *dangled from its socket,* and his face was *drenched with blood.*

**AUDITORY IMAGERY** There was the unmistakable *screech* of breaks and *thud* of a head hitting a dashboard.

**KINESTHETIC IMAGERY** As she started running, she noticed tiny *cramps* in her lower legs. Then, *shooting pains* began to work their way upward. She felt her knees literally *throbbing* with each step and the muscles in her thighs *burned* with the strain.

### WORD CHOICE: ANALOGY

The use of analogies also adds to your ability to be vivid and interesting. In addition, "analogies supply an equal sign between something strange and something familiar and are a powerful participatory persuasion tool."[56] For example, in a case where a slightly retarded defendant failed to register his rifle, a prosecutor could use vivid, interesting, and persuasive language by saying that virtually everyone knows you need a license to fish, to hunt, or to drive. It is inconceivable that anyone of any intelligence level would not know you also need a license to own a gun. Or Louis Nizer, in the libel case of *Quentin Reynolds v. Westbrook Pegler,* ridiculed the defendant's claim in order to have the jury laugh it out of the court. He said: "When an octopus is attacked by an enemy, it emits a black, inky fluid, and the water around it gets very black, and in the confusion, the octopus escapes." Nizer went on to identify all the false issues (Communism, nudity, stealing, etc.) raised by the defendant's attorney, comparing this issue-raising to the tactics of the octopus. The picture grew more ugly with each example. Later, Nizer said, "After a while I had only to wave my hand as if through dark water and say 'black fluid'-- and the illusion completed itself."[57]

Analogies are stirring because they link case information to actual experiences, knowledge, and ideas of jurors. The following attempt to characterize a case based on circumstantial evidence demonstrates the power of the analogy:

"This reminds me of my father reading *Robinson Crusoe* to me

> when I was a little boy. Remember when Robinson was on the island for such a long time all alone? One morning he went down to the beach and there was a footprint in the sand. Knowing that someone else was on the island, he was so overcome with emotion, he fainted.
>
> And why did he faint? Did he see a man? He woke to find Friday standing beside him, who was to be his friend on the island, but he didn't see Friday. Did he see a foot? No. He saw a footprint. That is, he saw marks in the sand, the kind of marks that are made by a human foot. He saw circumstantial evidence. But it was true, it was valid, it was compelling, as it would be to all of you. We live with it all of our lives. So let's look at the facts of this case -- for those tracks that prove the truth."[58]

This apt analogy was specifically designed to persuade the jury to accept a case that relied on circumstantial information.

In sum, you must be intensely aware of the impact of language on people, of how language influences the way impressions are formed. If you are not sensitive to language on this level, you increase the probability of creating unfavorable impressions about your case.[59] Here, for example, are two sentences that allow us to contrast wording: one is drab and colorless; the other is effective and lively.

> *Wrong Way:* "This is a dram shop lawsuit and my client, a quadriplegic, seeks damages against the defendant tavern."
>
> *Right Way:* "This is the case of a young mother of three small children who, for the rest of her natural life, will be paralyzed from the neck down because the defendant's tavern sold too much beer to a young driver."[60]

More will be said about the power of language in the courtroom in the section on closing arguments. However, remember always that *effective language and style are essential in any opening statement.*

## ATTENTION FACTORS

Persuasiveness depends on maintaining judge/jury interest and attention.[61] Of course, none of us pays complete attention to everything. Rather, we focus selectively on certain stimuli.[62] So do juries. Therefore, it is your job in the opening statement to obtain and retain juror interest. How? Several techniques[63] are noted below.

### ACTIVITY

Motion is definitely an attention-getter. *Activity* involves not only your own physical movements, but also the flow of your ideas. We have already suggested several ways in which narrative style facilitates verbal activity. The opening statement should march ahead crisply through the use of style. Do not spend much time dwelling on any one point. (See the section on Physical Delivery under Closing Arguments for detailed advice concerning physical movement.)

### PROXIMITY

If you refer to someone present in the courtroom, to some object close at hand, to the immediate litigation occasion, and/or to something that just happened, such as in voir dire, you are making use of another attention-getting device. For instance, if you tell the jury that the distance between the accused and the defendant was the same length as your counsel table, or if you tell them that the amount of time the fire burned was equal to the amount of time they just sat through voir dire, you are using *proximity*. Attention is drawn to what is immediate in the minds of the jury panel.

## FAMILIARITY

We all develop an interest in things we recognize from our everyday lives. When you mention those things to a jury, you are employing *familiarity* as an attention factor. Describing an intersection in town, a typical ice storm, shared values (such as respect for getting an education) or common problems (such as changing a tire) all trigger an "old friend" or "old nemesis" image in the minds of the jurors. This process is especially strong when the familiar is linked with something unfamiliar or unknown.

## CONFLICT

Forces that oppose each other compel attention, which is one reason so many people are drawn to sports events and political contests. Look for *conflicts* to emphasize. In a medical malpractice case, the struggle against disease by both the doctor and patient can be developed vividly. In an abuse case, the conflict between parent and child can be underscored. If at all possible, interject a sense of conflict into your opening statement, for it is a natural attention factor in a courtroom drama.

## SUSPENSE

One element that is particularly prominent in the art of good storytelling is *suspense*. You may achieve suspense in several ways. For instance, you may wish to build your story to a climax, keeping the jury in the dark about what happened until the end of the tale. Or you may use what is called "the parallel actions technique." For example, the accused and the victim in a manslaughter trial could be shown starting out from two separate places at two separate times. The actions of each would be followed separately, building toward the incident that brought the two of them together, in which one of them was killed.

## REALITY

This attention factor may be developed through the use of *visual aids.* Charts, photographs, models, drawings, PowerPoint images, animations, and the like not only give juries a verbal connection, but also make a visual connection to your claims. Visual aids impress more deeply than words alone. (Most jurisdictions permit visuals during the opening statement, although a few limit counsel to blackboard or flipchart drawings, which are rarely as attractive, interesting, or professional as the visual aids just mentioned.) In an auto accident case, for example, a diagram of the street location where the accident took place can help the jury see the path of the cars. Also, various medical model visual aids can be helpful. These should be prepared professionally in advance of the trial. They should be accurate and simple. Of course, they must be easily seen in detail, available for easy reference, and not be distracting. In using them, you must not block the audience's view of the material, and you must look at your audience, not primarily at the visual itself.

Thought should be given to how you can use a visual aid to your advantage and not to your disadvantage. For instance, in criminal cases, prosecutors may want to treat handguns as though they were cannons. As one counsel expressed it, "I once saw a prosecutor put a pen through the trigger part and hold it by the pen as if he were afraid of the gun. That gun became huge."[64] A visual aid becomes a disadvantage when there are simply too many words on it, as is often seen with documents or PowerPoint outlines. Too many words can reduce the impact of the visual aid.

Visuals help in getting the story across to the jury, especially if the story is complex. Research on the interaction between the mode in which the message is conveyed and the complexity of the message confirms this thesis. An experiment was conducted in which college students were asked to read, listen to an audiotape, or watch a videotape of a persuasive speech. Sometimes the message was simple and other times it was complex. The students were much more influenced by the simple message on audiotape or videotape. But, the complex message had more of an impact when it was in written form.[65] Following this finding, if you have a complex opening statement, you may want to outline the major events and issues in large written format on a visual aid so the jurors can graphically see the case before them while you are speaking. Or you may want to create a timeline for the jury to see so they can follow along as your story unfolds chronologically. But keep it as simple as possible with only a handful of key events pictured.

If prepared visual aids cannot be used for some reason, you may be able to use things already present in the courtroom as props. "While he was traveling 73 mph an hour, Mr. Powers was about as far away from Catherine as this window is from the back of the room." Many courtrooms seem to come to life as the visual element enhances the persuasiveness of the message.

## ATTENTION FACTORS AND THEMES

Although attention factors should be incorporated throughout your opening statement, it is especially important to carefully decide on the correct one(s) to use. Select those that you feel sure will grab the attention of the judge and jury, that will stick clearly in their minds, and that through the use of repetition, take them back to the case theme.

Evoke the precise image you want to portray and repeat that image with some frequency. When we think of facial tissue, the image is "Kleenex." When we think of a soft drink, the image is "Coke." When a judge or jury thinks about a case, the case should be linked to an attention factor and theme developed at the beginning of the opening statement and carried throughout the trial.

Here is an example from personal trial consulting experience. The plaintiff was claiming a fraudulent will had been drafted by the dead husband of the defendant. Not so, said the defense. The deceased left virtually his entire estate to a child from a second marriage. Why? It seems as though he wanted that child to receive a good education and he wanted his money to be spent toward that end. You might say he had a "fervor for education." Continuous use of the "fervor" theme throughout the trial became our slogan. Jurors reached a unanimous verdict for the defendant. The attention factor (familiarity with, and respect for education) linked to the case theme ("fervor for education") guided the jury's deliberations.

Visual aids are another attention factor that can be used to reinforce your theme. This helps you "communicate with double effectiveness – visually as well as verbally."[66] For example, suppose your theme is "We operated in good faith." Put these words at the top of a chart that lists all the things your client did that were right or appropriate. Stand near the chart every time you say that theme. Every time that theme comes up in opening statement, during the questioning of witnesses, or during closing argument, move to that same spot to constantly remind the jury of the good faith aspect of your case.

## DELIVERY

We have been discussing some presentational aspects of the opening statement that, when applied, will allow you to increase your ability to persuade. And there are some additional considerations. How long, for instance, should your opening statement be? What demeanor should you assume? Should notes be used? Should humor? Where should you physically position yourself during delivery? How important is non-verbal communication? Let's look at these aspects and a few others, too.

## LENGTH

Generally speaking, the opening statement should be as brief as possible. It should not be cursory, nor should it be verbose. Rather, it should be only long enough to make the necessary points and hold the judge's or jury's interest. You should "avoid flooding the jurors with details, facts, and figures, most of which will quickly fade out of existence. At the beginning of a trial, small details have no meaning."[67] Obviously, no set time limit can be placed on the opening statement. However, boring the jury by orating at great length and including too many details is counterproductive. Some counsel say 20 to 40 minutes is preferable;[68] others follow the guideline of 20 minutes per each week at trial.[69] Some federal courts are already asking attorneys to complete speeches to the jury in 20 minutes or less.

## DEMEANOR

Your opening statement should be delivered in a calm and natural manner. If nothing else, being natural and calm helps you *appear* confident and logical. A relaxed, friendly attitude is important. The delivery can even be conversational, as though your story were being told to a group of friends. The presentation of the opening statement is not the time for theatrics or high-flown oratory. Do not over-dramatize.

## USE OF NOTES

The opening statement should be delivered without reference to notes. If notes are used, they should be sparse and unobtrusive. In no instance should the opening be read from manuscript. It is important for you to maintain good eye contact with the judge or jury. Notes can be distracting. Furthermore, an opening statement delivered without notes or with very few notes (i.e., a brief outline) conveys the impression that you are sincere and thoroughly knowledgeable about the case.

## USE OF HUMOR

Even though many public speeches begin with a funny story, humor should be avoided in opening statements. Trials are a serious business for judges and jurors. The inclusion of a planned joke in the opening statement insults the jurors' belief that their task is a serious one. The joke can make you appear insincere, and it may make the jury feel uncomfortable. Of course, if something humorous inadvertently occurs, a warm smile or a chuckle from you is fine. In such situations, a cautious reaction to levity is permissible.

## USE OF POSITIONING

Where to physically position yourself in the courtroom during the opening statement is a basic decision you must make, if you have a choice in the matter. In most federal courts, you are required to stand behind a lectern, which severely limits your opportunity for body movement. Ideally, however, the opening statement should be given directly in front of, and a few feet away from, the jury. If you stand too close to the jurors, it tends to make them feel uncomfortable; if you stand too far away, your presence is reduced. Only speaking from one side of the jury box may give the impression that the people at the other end are being ignored. Tall, heavy, and loud lawyers should stand somewhat further away from the jury box than their short, thin, and soft-spoken counterparts. Otherwise, they might overpower the jury.

## NON-VERBAL COMMUNICATION

Although much of the legal literature about nonverbal communication and the opening statement frequently over-dramatizes the subject, there are some basics that should be kept in mind as rules of thumb. Of particular note are eye contact, gestures and movement.

You must maintain eye contact with the judge or with all members of the jury as you deliver your opening statement. Even though you feel comfortable doing so, it is not a good idea to concentrate eye contact solely on those jurors who look sympathetic to your cause. Those who do not receive eye contact from you will perceive you as uncomfortable and untrustworthy. Furthermore, you can learn a lot from watching all the jury members' eyes. If jurors roll their eyes during a part of the opening statement, you may well be into a topic area that you must work hard to prove. If jurors drop their gaze from yours, little is to be concluded because this reaction is natural when one is in strange surroundings. It is also a natural response to any attempt at persuasion.

The pioneer study on reflex action of pupils found that sudden widening or narrowing of pupils could be related to attitudes and that, generally, our pupils dilate when we see or hear something we like, contract when we see or hear something distasteful, and remain unchanged when we are indifferent.[70] Anthropologist Edward Hall notes that Arabs have known about pupil response for years and "since people can't control the response of their eyes…many Arabs…wear dark glasses, even indoors."[71] During the opening statement, you can observe jurors' pupils (although it is often difficult to see them) to better understand their reactions to what you are saying.

Gestures and movements are extremely important dimensions of nonverbal communication and you should give them considerable attention. If you constantly point at the jury with your pen, for example, or twirl your Phi Beta Kappa key, or scratch your nose, or jingle the change in your pocket, you are using mannerisms that distract your audience. Gestures and movements that are too effusive or repetitive, unrelated to the message content, uncoordinated, and indefinite will broadcast a poor image.

Standing with your arms folded while speaking is unimpressive. If you need support, it is better to lean against a table or chair than to use your own body for support by crossing your arms against your midsection. Pacing back and forth in front of the judge or jury is also a bad idea. So is rooting yourself in one spot and never moving. If a lectern is required, you should move around to one side of it, or occasionally go to the front of it, so that the lectern does not "swallow you up" and render you unimpressive. Effective movement occurs either during breaks in thought (transitions) or when you are stressing a particularly important point.

Poor physical delivery is often the result of nervousness and lack of adequate preparation. It is best to be your natural self. If you are nervous, try hard not to concentrate on being nervous. Forget about it. If you keep your mind on what you are saying, how it is being said will then be self-corrective. Also, you might ask a partner or colleague to watch this aspect of your presentation and give you feedback shortly afterwards. If video is available, observe yourself on tape and note ways to improve.

## TONE OF VOICE

Throughout your opening statement your voice should be pleasant and moderate, but audible. Pace is crucial. The speech should be neither rushed nor plodding. A monotone or steady pitch is dull and will not uplift the jury. A voice therapist has noted that many a juror has considered an argument weak simply because both voice and manner worked against the speaker.[72]

## OPENINGS TO THE BENCH

Should an opening to the bench be treated any differently than an opening to a jury? The answer is "not really." You can be more legalistic in an opening before a judge. The judge, unlike the jury, may occasionally interrupt your opening to ask for clarification.

There have been times, in fact, when the opening in a bench trial has become a running colloquy between the judge and one or both attorneys. Fundamentally, however, there is no difference between opening to the court and opening to a jury.[73] All of the principles of presentation reviewed in this book apply in non-jury trials as well.

## THE OPENING STATEMENT: PREPARATION

After the facts are gathered, the issues decided, and the witnesses coached, you should carefully and thoroughly prepare a written outline for the opening statement. Such advance planning is critical. The judge or jury should never be given the idea that you have not devoted any prior contemplation to your opening address.[74]

At times, it is advisable to write out and edit your opening statement word for word or with a detailed outline to see what it looks like. This writing should be done just before the trial begins. You should review it carefully in order to alter substance or approach, if necessary. Alterations may be advisable after assessing the jurors selected to hear the case. You may even have to alter the outline *during* your actual presentation. However, writing out your opening statement in full or outline form before trial forces you to give it the serious consideration it deserves.

Once you have the outline or written text polished, practice giving your opening statement aloud, first with notes and later without them (or at least using nothing more than a "crib" card containing a few cue words at most.) Rehearsals increase your delivery proficiency. Detailed knowledge of a case is not the equivalent of stating it to others persuasively. Practicing aloud can be done before relatives, friends, or other (unbiased) lay persons in order to obtain feedback and helpful criticism. Practicing with an audio or videotape recorder can also be an invaluable experience.

## RECOMMENDATIONS FOR PRESENTING THE OPENING STATEMENT

### RECOMMENDATIONS FOR ATTORNEYS ON BOTH SIDES OF THE CASE

- Explain technical, medical, and legal terms in lay language
- Use simple words instead of complex words; short sentences, not complex sentences
- Use imagery to create vivid pictures for your audience
- Appeal to all the senses (sight, sound, touch, taste, muscular sensation, organic feeling) in some way
- Think of analogies to make unclear information clear and interesting to your audience
- Keep your ideas moving; tell your story crisply
- Use proximity (to some object in the courtroom) and familiarity (something everyone knows) to hold audience interest
- Create a sense of conflict and suspense as you tell your opening statement story
- Use creative, informative, and dramatic visual aids
- Connect your attention factor(s) to your theme(s); repeat this connection throughout the trial
- Keep your opening statement as brief as possible

- Use minimal notes or no notes at all
- Avoid inserting humor
- If permitted, deliver your opening statement directly in front of, and a few feet away from, the jury
- Maintain eye contact with your audience
- Avoid distracting gestures and movements
- Develop variety of voice tone; avoid speaking at the same rate, pitch, and volume

### AS A PLAINTIFF'S ATTORNEY OR PROSECUTOR, BE VERBALLY ASSERTIVE AND DIRECT

- Use affirming words such as *very, certain,* and *definitely*
- Use strong image words such as *collision, crash, wreck,* or *tragedy*
- Refer to damages as *compensation* for a wrongdoing

### AS A DEFENSE ATTORNEY, BE POLITE, AMBIGUOUS, AND VERBALLY HESITANT

- Say *please, I hope, I think,* and *maybe*
- Use abstractions such as *accident, mishap,* or *one of those things*
- Avoid unnecessary and disruptive phrases such as the "evidence will show that"... or "we expect to prove that..."
- Refer to damages as *winning an award*

# PART TWO

# CLOSING ARGUMENTS

## THE RHETORIC OF THE CLOSING ARGUMENT

Little quantified information is available concerning the importance of the final argument. Some behavioral research[75] indicates (and some practitioners believe) that the final argument is the most important single feature of any lawsuit.[76] Others think that lawsuits are won during the trial, not at the conclusion of it.[77] Almost all lawyers agree, however, that lawsuits can be lost by incoherent or exaggerated closing arguments.[78] One of the earliest studies investigating jurors' reactions to summations found that the closing argument was an "important" factor influencing the jurors' opinions and, for some of the jurors, the summing up was the most effective stage of the entire trial.[79]

On occasion, and usually before bench trials rather than jury trials, lawyers waive closing arguments. Sometimes, the trial judge dispenses with final arguments since the trial briefs are considered adequate to present the parties' positions.[80] However, in jury trials, waiving the closing argument is not a good idea. After all, jurors expect to hear a climactic, clarifying summation at the close of trials that stimulates recall of key facts. Waiving may be misconstrued as a sign of weakness. We should, then, examine the closing argument as closely as we did the opening statement.

## THE CLOSING ARGUMENT: RECENCY

In some jurisdictions, the defense speaks first in closing, and the plaintiff or prosecutor speaks last. In other jurisdictions, the plaintiff attorney or the prosecutor speaks first and then replies in rebuttal to the defense's closing argument. In both situations, the plaintiff or prosecutor gets the last word in closing arguments. Of course, the plaintiff or prosecutor also got the first chance to speak in opening statements. Is there an advantage in speaking last?

### RESEARCH ON RECENCY

The so-called recency effect indicates *that the last statement uttered in a communication is often the most memorable and influential statement.* Research on this effect shows that there is some advantage in speaking last at trial. One study, for instance, found that when 160 undergraduates read jury trial excerpts, a significant recency effect appeared regarding both their opinion of the case and their retention of information. When prosecutors spoke last, their words were more impressive and better retained; when defense attorneys spoke last, their words were better remembered and most persuasive.[81] (Note: Recency even tends to increase in strength if there is some delay between the two closing arguments.)

Research conducted since the late fifties has consistently confirmed the recency phenomenon.[82] Many believe that prosecutors and plaintiffs are distinctly favored in the trial format by virtue of the fact that they give the last speech, thereby leaving their arguments uppermost in the jurors' minds.[83] If you were conducting the defense, you might want to discuss the research findings on recency and then ask the judge or jury to not let the last speech heard influence them unduly.

## RECENCY AND PRIMACY

You will recall that the psychological principle of primacy holds that what is said first and accepted as reasonable or appealing is difficult to counter. The primacy advantage rests with the prosecutor or plaintiff's attorney. The same prosecutor or plaintiff's attorney benefits from the psychological principle of recency. As a result, some thought-provoking questions have been raised about trial format. "How does the... order [of the trial] which combines both primacy and recency effects balance the burden of proof? Or does it offer a balancing effect at all? Is there an unfair advantage for the plaintiff or prosecutor?"[84] These questions are difficult to answer, and so far we have only speculation about the issue. Some defense attorneys argue that primacy and recency effects have actually shifted the burden of proof to the defense. Research on this matter is badly needed.

## THE CLOSING ARGUMENT: GOALS

Closing arguments tie together everything that went on during a trial while separating the meaningful from the trivial. They bring together "all the disparate elements of the evidence produced at the trial and mold them into a simple, understandable theory of your case. Ideally, the closing argument should not be an abrupt change of direction, but instead should be a fitting conclusion to the continuum that began with your opening statement."[85] Since the evidentiary part of the trial may appear to your audience to be disjointed, confusing, and even contradictory, you are now given an opportunity to bring it all back together into a logical relationship, weaving the testimony, documents, and other evidence into the cohesive story presented originally in your opening statement.[86]

Neither the judge nor lay witnesses may offer their opinions regarding the meaning and significance of the evidence. That job is left up to you. Furthermore, this is the point in the trial when you are trying to persuade a judge or jury to adopt your version of the case facts. Your summation should be an argumentative speech designed to focus on and clarify certain issues that will guide the judge or jury in their deliberations by giving them arguments they can use. While it is true that you are involved in persuasion throughout a jury trial, the most obviously persuasive part of the process is the closing argument.

Some people call the closing argument the summation. Indeed, the term *summation* is used here as well. What happens in this part of the trial, however, must go beyond summarizing the evidence. Argument is not a mere summary; argument is persuasion addressed to the thorniest problems a case can present.[87] It is the ammunition with which you will arm jurors to argue your case in deliberations.

Summations nearly always differ between judge and jury trials. For instance, before a jury, counsel is precluded from urging any personal interpretation of the law; whereas an attorney in a bench trial is allowed to argue matters of law.[88]

Occasionally, a judge may interrupt counsel during the presentation of a closing argument to pose questions and engage in debate. When such questioning occurs, you should address yourself to the question (or comment) even if it interrupts the train of thought.[89] Then you should return to the planned argument, unless you have been interrupted several times because the judge is hinting at where you should be spending your time and effort. In that case, you should follow the judge's "hint" throughout a bench trial summation. You may also use more technical language in a bench trial and be less repetitious than you are with a jury.[90] Be it judge or jury, the goal of a closing argument should remain the same: *to clarify and to persuade.*

## THE CLOSING ARGUMENT: CONTENT AND STRUCTURE

Wide latitude is usually given when making your summation, although you are not free to say merely anything you wish. Some argument is improper. Let's take a look at some of the common boundaries that may be violated.

### IMPROPER CONDUCT

Asserting a new fact or point in the closing argument that was not offered during the presentation of evidence constitutes improper conduct. For example, prosecutors risk objections if they say, "The defense has made a big point of the absence of bloodstains on the victim's car seat. Perhaps I should have brought in the bloodstained cushion." Because the existence of the bloodstained cushion had not been put in evidence, it should not have been mentioned in the closing argument. It is also improper conduct to distort evidence by misquoting, by quoting out of context, or by omitting unfavorable information.[91]

Blatantly appealing for sympathy and making inflammatory appeals to prejudice and passion also constitute inappropriate conduct. Displaying emotion in the closing argument is permitted, but appealing to prejudice is not. A prejudicial slur by a defense counsel might be something like this: "Here we have an avowed atheist seeking to prevent praying in the school that our God-fearing, tax-paying neighbors are paying for." Other forms of improper argument appeal to racial or religious prejudice, nationality or regionalism, or prejudice regarding the wealth or poverty of the parties in litigation.[92]

Still another infraction is the "golden rule" doctrine, in which a jury is asked to put themselves in a client's position, thereby being invited to disregard their oaths and become nonobjective viewers of the evidence.[93] Plaintiff's attorney cannot say, "Imagine yourself in the position of this young woman who lost her home, her belongings, and her beloved pet." However, you can properly remind a jury of any promises they made during their voir dire, promises such as setting aside bias and giving fair consideration to the issues and the evidence.

One final example of improper conduct in summation is discourteous or insinuating remarks about opposing counsel. One winning appeal was based on the reference by plaintiff's attorney in closing to defense counsel as someone who had spent his entire life only representing rich corporations and, as such, could not see any plaintiff's claim as just. The appeals court found the remark to be prejudicial.[94]

To conclude, you are forbidden from making improper arguments in your summation. Sometimes, these remarks are grounds for reversal, particularly if the improper conduct was the basis of an objection by opposing counsel at the time of the infraction.[95] Objections, however, should be used sparingly, and only if the alleged infraction appears serious. Objections that are overruled foster the impression that objecting counsel is deliberately interfering with the opponent's case presentation. Although what has been said here may make it seem as though you need to exercise extreme caution in the closing argument, such is not the case. Justice Brown has said: "If every remark made by counsel outside of the testimony were grounds for a reversal, relatively few verdicts would stand, since in the ardor of advocacy, and in the excitement of a trial, even the most experienced counsel are occasionally carried away by this temptation."[96]

We have been talking in this section about what should be *omitted* from closings. What, then, should appear in an ideal closing argument? Because structure and order help to achieve balance and reduce confusion and frustration,[97] summations should be well organized and contain certain expected content in order to make it easier for your listeners to remember your message. The impact of a closing is significantly related to its content and structure. Let's now consider the structure of the closing argument: the introduction ("tell them what you are going to tell them"), the body ("tell them"), and the conclusion ("tell them what you told them").

## THE INTRODUCTION

In a few, not-too-effusive sentences at the beginning of your summation, you might say, "Good afternoon. We have now reached the point in the trial where closing arguments will be presented. This is the time when the lawyers will remind you what their cases are all about." An informative statement of this nature can be followed by a brief word of thanks to the judge and jury for their attentiveness and patience. What you are doing here is expressing sincerity to your audience. After all, sincerity is comfortable and flattering. Ingratiation is the rhetorical tactic of making yourself attractive to an audience. Successful ingratiation results in esteem with your jury, and may bias them in your favor. But if any attempt at ingratiating yourself with the jury is too obvious, the strategy can backfire and be seen as manipulation. Showing sincere appreciation should result in a judge and jury being more receptive to what follows in your summation than if you immediately stand up and begin arguing your case.[98] The dilemma of the person practicing ingratiation is knowing where to draw the line. Common sense must prevail. But keep your opening sentences very brief. What you want to turn attention to quickly is your summation of the strong points of your case.

The introduction is the place where you should restate the theme of your case. What was this case all about? You should not delve into details at this time; simply remind the jury of the basic theme you developed earlier. For instance, a theme based on safety and the value of a meaningful human life is found in this statement, "Calvin Bond will never be able to use his right arm for the rest of his life. His prospects of ever leading a normal life were ruined when an armed man entered Mr. Bond's clothing store and shot him in the arm after taking all the money out of his cash register." In other words, "shoot your silver bullets during the first moments of your summation speech. These opening lines should be confident, authentic, absolutistic, and conclusive."[99] It is extremely important that when this short introduction is finished, you have the complete attention of the jury focused on the paramount theme encompassing the message to follow.

## THE BODY

Five essential matters concerning the heart of the closing are covered in the body of most summations. These are: *a statement concerning the issues, a statement on the burden of proof, a review of key evidence, some review of adverse evidence, and a statement as to how the facts apply to the law.*

## THE ISSUES

All cases should boil down to a *few determinative issues that* form the game plan for the case. The issue or issues an attorney stands on, whether legal, factual, or ethical, must be made clear. Your stance governs the nature of inquiry. For example, if you took a position based on a legal issue, you might talk about considering all aspects of safety regulations as they are outlined in the relevant statutes. If you stand on a factual issue, your question to the jury might be something like, "Did it happen or didn't it?" If your stance is ethical, you would say, "The basic issue here is, Will we or will we not let a slumlord get away with renting firetraps to poor people?" Here is an interesting way to view the concept:

> An issue is a key or pivotal question of fact or philosophy raised by the contentions of the party. For example, in a simple intersectional case, the key issue would be which party had the green light. If the plaintiff had witnesses establishing the issue, then he should stress this issue. The defendant may then defend his case on collateral issues... or side issues on which the defense can win.[100]

An issue (say, for example, an eyewitness identification of an alleged assailant) is not to be confused with the case theme (safety and the value of a meaningful human life). As noted, *themes are central motivating ideas that pervade an entire case; issues are major points to be supported by the evidence.* Highlighting the issues in the closing argument means that you refer to the pleadings that started the case.

While the lawyer for the plaintiff tries to simplify these main issues, the defense attorney often scatters attention over several points, especially when its case on the main issues is weak. Successful defense attorneys often employ the "how about this, and how about that" tactic. For example, "If the injury were as serious as claimed, why did the plaintiff decline first aid on the spot?" or "Why hasn't he missed a softball game since the accident?" This strategy is intended to raise incremental doubt in the mind of the judge or jurors, thereby causing them to find for the defense.

The entire body of the summation should be organized around the issues themselves. No matter what type of issues or how many issues are chosen, they should not be organized on a witness-by-witness pattern. This can be repetitious and tedious. But neither should the issues be summarized chronologically as they were in the storytelling opening statement.

The body of the closing argument should begin with a simple road map summary and subsequent development of the issues. The following illustrates a good basic beginning to the body of a summation:

> The judge will instruct you that you should return a verdict for Jane Porter if you believe four things: First, that the defendant either drove at an excessive speed or was intoxicated; second, that his conduct was negligent; third, that Jane Porter sustained injuries as a result of such negligence; and fourth, that the driver was operating the Ajax Company truck within the scope of his employment by Ajax. These are the issues you must decide.[101]

There are two particular aspects about the use of key issues in closing argument that you should consider: the number of issues raised and the order in which they are raised. The number of issues introduced should definitely be restricted. Research suggests that there is an upper limit to the number of issues or arguments an attorney can present and still have persuasive effect. In one experiment, subjects were exposed to anywhere from 1 to 16 prosecutorial arguments.[102] The subjects were then asked to rate their strength of belief in the defendant's guilt. Ratings of guilt increased steadily as the number of prosecutorial issues increased up to about 10 arguments. Thereafter, the effect of adding more arguments was negligible. The most persuasive effects took place when between 7 and 10 arguments were used.

In what order should the issues be presented? Should you begin with weaker arguments and build to the strongest one, or should you start with the strongest argument for your side and then cover the rest in descending order? After studying research in communication and social psychology, one scholar concludes that "arguing 'climax-anticlimax,' which is going from strong to weak, ... is ... the most persuasive pattern for argument."[103] *Your strongest argument should be stated first.* If you wait to put your strongest issue last, you may be facing a skeptical jury that has been asked to accept weaker positions in the case first.

## BURDEN OF PROOF

After highlighting the issues, you should discuss the burden of proof. The proof required to establish or refute conviction or right of recovery needs your explanation and interpretation. In a civil case, as you explain "preponderance of the evidence," you may want to draw the scales of justice on a blackboard or use your arms as the scales, pointing out that a slight tilting in your favor, no matter how *slight,* is sufficient to carry the burden of proof.[104] From the plaintiff's point of view, jurors must understand that "beyond a reasonable doubt" carries with it a greater burden of proof standard than having to believe in that story by just a "preponderance of the evidence." By way of analogy, in a baseball game a team can win by a 3-2 margin (preponderance of the evidence); the score does not have to be 3-0 (no reasonable doubt).

As defense, remind the jury that the plaintiff's attorney or the prosecutor has the burden of proof. In a criminal case, you should refer to as many "reasonable doubts" as possible, and not to a single reasonable doubt. To do this, you could review the testimony from your opposition for foggy memories, inconsistencies, or lack of evidence.[105] For example, you might say, "I wonder why Jane Doe forgot what time it was or what the weather was like that day." Or "I wonder why John Smith said in his deposition that he heard nothing, but yesterday in court he said he heard quite a bit." Or "I wonder why the victim was unable to identify his attacker on the day of the assault, but in court he pointed to the defendant." What you are doing is creating reasonable doubts. Your opponent will attempt to offset this approach by recounting, point by point, how he or she has met each responsibility.

## REVIEW OF KEY EVIDENCE

Key evidence must be reviewed in the closing argument. This evidence amplifies and supports your position on the contested issues. For example, a contested issue might be whether or not a defendent was under the influence of alcohol. The main purpose of providing detail during this review of key evidence is to resolve the contested issues. The detail ought to show that your witnesses had consistent facts, demonstrated common sense, and were credible. You might also show that you had the greater quantity of evidence.

Review and analysis of the evidence should not be tediously discussed witness-by-witness. Instead, the material should be categorized under each of the pertinent issues.[106] An issue-by-issue summary is sometimes referred to as "marshalling the evidence." In outline form, a contested issue argument at this point in the body of your summation might look like this:

Statement of issue
Summary of relevant evidence
Discussion
Statement of next issue
Summary of evidence relevant to that issue
Discussion, etc.[107]

Going over all of your own witnesses' testimony in great detail again is a waste of time. Only the essential facts need to be analyzed as each statement of issue is developed by evidence or facts. What do these facts mean? How do they relate to the issues? Are the sources of these facts credible? Why are the facts probably true? How do they fit together as a story? Is there a preponderance of the facts for your side?

As the questions are answered, you should avoid saying, "I believe the evidence shows that John Doe is guilty of this crime." Such language sounds hopeful and apologetic. More positive and persuasive phrasing would be, "The evidence convincingly establishes that John Doe is guilty of this crime."

In addition, you should not be a simple fact-reviewing machine as you develop the issues. Rather, you should explain how you get from the evidence to a claim or conclusion. For example, you might say, "Witness A said that fact 2 exists. From that we can infer that fact 3 also exists." (The basis of such an inference is common experience.) Or you might say, "The testimony of Dr. Vasquez was that the defendant's semen was found in Molly. I am trying to establish the claim that the defendant was Molly's attacker. Now, how does that testimony relate to the issue?" Answering this question exposes your inference-making process. Explicit reasoning helps make cases clearer and more convincing to juries and judges alike.[108] As two analysts of the closing argument conclude:

> ...We believe that it is not enough for the lawyer to merely lay out the information and hope the jury will arrive at a logical decision. Wishful thinking is not enough. Rather, he or she must realize that since other factors come into play, it is up to the attorney to analyze the available information for the jury. It is up to the attorney to delineate the steps that go into the analysis so that the jury will be able to answer in their own minds the question "Why?" Why did they arrive at a particular verdict?[109]

## REVIEW OF ADVERSE EVIDENCE

After key evidence is marshaled under each major issue, you must decide how extensively to discuss the lack of credibility and sufficiency of adverse evidence. On the one hand, it seems clear that the positive points of your case should be emphasized, and little time should be spent pointing out deficiencies in the case of the opposition lest the trial turn into a picayune debating match. On the other hand, argument that presents and then refutes a counterargument can be persuasive, particularly when the audience is familiar with the issues on both sides, as it certainly is in a trial.[110] Such "two-sided" arguments build speaker credibility because their use conveys candor, fairness,[111] intelligence, and the ability to argue both sides.[112] In court, a two-sided argument is more effective than a strictly one-sided evidence review,[113] although the thrust of a summation certainly should be on the positive aspects of one's own case.

## APPLICATION OF THE LAW TO THE FACTS

You may want to comment on *how the facts apply to relevant legal principles.* This does not mean arguing the law, but rather showing how the law that the judge will present in the jury instructions applies to the issues and facts at hand. You will want to tell the jury that the instructions are those of the court and not of the parties in the case. Then, you should proceed to argue the elements of the cause of action in relation to the evidence you have presented.

For example, what requirements have to be met to prove assault, and have these requirements been met? As a prosecutor, you will want to show that all the legal requirements have been met. As a defense lawyer, you will focus on those elements you contend have not been met.

It is at this point that you must decide whether your case is strong on facts but weak on law, or the opposite. For example, if as plaintiff's counsel you have a case strong on facts but weak on law, you should appeal to the emotion of jurors. Since it is difficult to tie emotional appeals to the law, and since case facts generally have some emotional story linked to them, the focus of the case should be on the story. Likewise, in the same case, defense counsel should appeal to less emotional jurors who also have less tolerance for violation of procedural rules. Those jurors would not be as much involved in the emotionalism of the incident as they would be in the language of the law as it applies to this case.

## ADDITIONAL ADVICE

Two points of advice concerning the body of closing arguments are worth taking to heart. (Actually, both of these points apply to your opening statement as well.) First, *case weaknesses should be admitted* by the side that has them. Jurors appreciate and respect such candor and honesty.[114] Of course, as damage control, the insignificance of these weaknesses should be emphasized. In like manner, any unfavorable information should be quickly mitigated.[115]

Second, *explicit logic should be used by the plaintiff's attorney or prosecutor, but implicit logic should be used by the defense attorney.* The difference between explicit and implicit arguments is really one of degree, not of kind.[116] Explicit argument: "We cannot place any faith in the testimony of Catherine Doyle." Implicit argument: "Can you really trust the testimony of Catherine Doyle?" Or a plaintiff's attorney could answer the inevitable question in the minds of a jury: "All right, Counselor, we understand your point.

Now, what do you want us to do about it?" by saying: "Ladies and gentlemen, I ask you to make a decision for which you can feel proud. I ask you to give Sally Miller decency and justice by giving her 100 percent of what she deserves, and that is the sum of $200,000." Meanwhile, the defense attorney should say: "Do you really think Sally Miller deserves $200,000? In fact do you really think she deserves anything at all?" The art of developing appropriate conclusions is essential to presenting closing arguments that are logically persuasive.

## THE CONCLUSION

The conclusion should bring your closing argument to a resounding climax. This is where most of the emotional appeal should appear.[117] The conclusion of each summation should be concise and forceful; this is the time for eloquence. Though the following example might seem overdramatic to some attorneys, the concluding remarks of defense attorney Sir Edward Marshall in the *Greenwood* murder case display the kind of power necessary at this point:

> Your verdict is final, necessarily final. Science can do a great deal; these men with their mirrors, multipliers, and milligrams, can tell you to the ten-thousandth or millionth part of a grain the constituents of the human body. Science has enabled us to talk from here to thousands of miles away without any intervening wire or visible means of communication. Science has enabled us to kill thousands by obnoxious gases, and can enable us to blow ourselves to pieces with one little explosive. But science cannot do one thing: that is to find the vital spark which converts inert clay into a human being. Once the life is gone out of a man, be it as a result of a jury's verdict of murder, or be it by any other cause, life is at an end, and no power of science can replace it. I ask you to remember the scene in "Othello" where the jealous Moor made up his mind to kill Desdemona. Othello enters Desdemona's chamber, makes up his mind to kill her relentlessly, for he believes her to be unchaste,

> and seeing her lying there he thinks of the effect of killing her as compared with putting out her light, and says: "Put out the light," and then he puts out the light. Are you by your verdict going to put out that light? Gentlemen of the Jury, I demand at your hands the life and liberty of Harold Greenwood.

The last few words of your closing argument said to a jury should be strong ones. Melvin Belli says that the last few lines might even be memorized.[118] In show business, entertainers try for strong finishes with what they call tag lines. You should do likewise. The "put out the light" reference, combined with the awesome power a jury has on its shoulders, constituted an effective tag line for Sir Edward Marshall.

## SUMMATION LENGTH

How long should a closing argument last? In the days of Daniel Webster and Clarence Darrow, when the trial served as a form of public entertainment, summations often consumed two or three days.[119] Today, closing arguments generally go from a few minutes to several hours. One hour, or on rare occasions two hours, is about as long as a summation should go.[120] Though speed is not of the essence, eloquence is. No hard-and-fast rule can be established regarding the length of an effective summation. The complexity of the case, combined with your speaking ability, ought to be factors in determining how long your closing argument should last.

With increasing frequency, courts are establishing the time allocated for closing arguments. Equal time, such as 20 minutes apiece, is given to both sides. A bailiff keeps the time and informs the lawyers when they have but a few minutes remaining. In these instances, pacing is very important. If possible, you should practice to adapt to the time limit. And in court, you should leave your watch where you can unobtrusively see it so the time can be observed.

## RECOMMENDATIONS FOR THE CONTENT AND STRUCTURE OF CLOSING ARGUMENTS

- You must not assert a new fact or distort evidence
- You must not make inflammatory appeals to emotions and prejudices
- You must not ask the jurors to put themselves in your client's position
- You should not be discourteous to your opposition
- Begin with a brief statement of appreciation and an explanation of what you are about to do
- Reintroduce your case theme
- The plaintiff's attorney or prosecutor should preview the few key issues the jury will have to decide; the defense attorney may want to reply by explaining the complications of the case
- Organize the speech around the key issues, not chronologically; signpost each issue

- Place your strongest issue first, your next strongest issue last, and the remaining issues in between them
- Explain the burden of proof
- Review important evidence as each issue is developed
- Explain to your audience what you are inferring from the evidence presented
- Engage in a limited discussion of your adversary's evidence
- Show how the facts of the case relate to the law as outlined in the judge's instructions
- Admit to any case weakness you might have, and note the insignificance of these weaknesses
- As a plaintiff's attorney or prosecutor, use explicit logic; as a defense attorney, use implicit language
- The last section of your closing argument is the time for oratory and eloquence

## THE CLOSING ARGUMENT: EMOTIONAL APPEALS

Appealing to the emotions in argument is often denounced. Perhaps it should be denounced if it goes overboard. However, while exaggerated emotional appeals are to be avoided, some emotionalism in summations is strategically wise. Why? Because you are really asserting a point of view; you are urging belief into the stories you tell. "Dry appeals to the pure intellect with no emotional content are not very persuasive."[121] Therefore, the basic elements of salesmanship, emotional appeal included, apply to the summation. Emotion in the closing argument can take several different forms. Those we will examine here include dramatic presentation, exciting use of visual aids, direct psychological appeals, and the use of vivid language.

### DRAMATIC PRESENTATION

One form of emotionalism in the summation is the dramatic presentation. Only lawyers capable of using dramatic voice and manner should try this approach. Those without this skill appear phony. Dramatic presentations may involve modulating your voice from a whisper to a shout or parading around the courtroom and playing center stage. The use of such dramatic tactics will be discussed further in subsequent sections.

### VISUAL AIDS

Emotions can also be aroused, and attention gained, through an exciting use of visual aids, not only in closing argument, but also throughout the trial. The Rand Corporation found that 55% to 75% of information is understood and retained over a 24-hour period when presented both orally and visually. But only 15% to 25% is understood and retained when presented only orally.[122]

If you ignore the use of visual aids, you ignore a whole framework of persuasion in psychology.[123] As one vivid example, a defense lawyer could dramatize the idea of contributory negligence by tearing a sheet of paper into a large piece and a tiny one, and then holding them up for contrast, saying, "If my client was negligent... (showing them the large piece of paper), and the plaintiff was negligent... (showing the small piece), then under the law, it is the sworn duty of this jury to find my client not guilty. It is not a matter of weighing which one was more negligent. Before he can collect ten cents, the plaintiff must prove that he, himself, was not even guilty of that much negligence (again showing the small piece of paper)."[124]

All kinds of visual aids are permitted in the closing argument. They can be used to communicate the case theme and issues to the jury. For example, you might list the elements of the cause of action on a chart or blackboard and cross out or erase the uncontested ones.[125] Charts can be used to show damage computations, chronology of events, lists of witnesses, and so on. Diagrams or animations of accident scenes can recreate the movements and relative positions of the parties. The displaying of real evidence, such as the murder weapon in a homicide, is an effective persuasive technique. Tangible, visual material involves the eye and is a powerfully persuasive tool when used in the closing argument.[126]

## PSYCHOLOGICAL APPEALS

Another form of emotionalism is a direct psychological appeal. Sir Edward Marshall provided us with an example of the emotionally charged psychological appeal of fear and sympathy in the *Greenwood* case. Such psychological appeals should be aimed directly at the value systems and attitudes of the jurors. Value systems include such familiar ingredients as love of family, justice, Puritan morality, freedom, honesty, success, work, practicality, rationality, quantity (bigness, speed), safety, comfort, generosity, patriotism, responsibility, conformity, fairness, and so forth. Attitudes related to these values are complex mixtures that reveal how one feels, what one knows or believes, and how one is predisposed to act.

When appealing to attitudes and values, you must try to "anchor" compatibility between yourself, your audience, and the decision that is being urged. Anchoring as a technique is based upon consistency theory.[127] Consistency theory's major premise is that people are more comfortable with consistency than inconsistency. We strive for balance in our lives, and any information that creates dissonance causes us to become tense.[128] The information that flows from your case must be consistent with (i.e., anchored into) your jurors' basic belief systems. The following offers sound advice regarding the anchoring technique:

> The point to remember is that if you can anchor your case to one of these widely accepted foundations you will make it difficult for your opponent to sway the jury because their belief about your case cannot be altered without changing the other beliefs to which it is anchored. Since changing two or more interlocking beliefs is more difficult than changing an isolated belief, successful anchoring creates resistance to the persuasive attempts of your opponent. Obviously, the more firmly your case is anchored in the deeply held values and beliefs of the jurors, the more resistant they will be to counter-persuasion.[129]

Emotion resides in the attitudes and values of the jurors. When these attitudes and values are tapped, people are likely to be moved into action. Here, for instance, is a psychological appeal to the value of life: "I am proud that our country places a higher value on life than any other country in the world. You judge a civilization by what it thinks of human life. I believe that it is a high mark of our civilization that we hold to the principle that life is our most precious and valuable commodity. Our forefathers thought so when they said that each person is entitled to life, liberty, and the pursuit of happiness." A common appeal of defense lawyers is to ask a jury to leave sympathy out of the case and then ask for a fair trial. Such an appeal to fairness is like asking a jury to endorse motherhood: the appeal is virtually unattackable. As long as the rhetoric is not condescending, any appeal to anchor values can help to shape belief in the closing argument.

## VIVID LANGUAGE USE

Some authors who write about persuasion explain that vivid language is the key to the whole process of using psychological appeals successfully.[130] After reviewing years of research of the Duke University Law and Language Project, an analyst concluded: "The matter in which a person speaks may be as important as what he says in shaping the conclusions of his audiences."[131] Numerous other studies link speaker credibility, audience interest, and language choice.[132] The idea is to use vivid language in order to appeal to listeners' perceptions and keep their attention on the speaker's message. Vivid language causes humans to think and deal in mental pictures. The opposite of vivid language – abstraction -- is not likely to elicit the mental pictures you desire. The words *book, relative, insect,* and *contraceptive device* are abstract; the words *paperback novel, devoted father, killer bee,* and *condom* are more concrete and vivid.

Vivid words evoke feelings. Consequently, word choice has much to do with persuasion. Note the difference between saying "a wound that is oozing pus" and "a lesion that is suppurating." The first version captures attention. Writers on style urge the use of vivid words to evoke sensory images.

**SENSORY APPEAL** In closing argument, you have occasion to choose vivid words for pain, suffering, anguish, worry, fear, grief, embarrassment, shame, and the like. Words such as *hearty, laugh, glowing health, smash-up, mangled,* and *pounding* evoke images more effectively than words such as *satisfactory, negligent,* *incident*, and *direct result*. Why? Because they appeal to the senses. Sensory language is to the lawyer what the rainbow of colors is to the painter.[133] The lawyer who says, "Joe heard a piercing screech followed by a loud crash" appeals to our auditory sense. The lawyer who says, "Jane saw a green Volvo run the red light and smash the small brown Toyota broadside" appeals to our visual sense. The lawyer who says, "Jack felt scared to death and helpless when he realized he was trapped in his car" appeals to our kinesthetic (internal feeling) sense. Attorneys who, in closing arguments, use sensory language will, in turn, appeal to the sensory channels of the jury. Notice how visual imagery is used in this portion of a closing argument concerning the accidental blinding of a man with five children. Visual imagery is used in the first paragraph; kinesthetic in the second; auditory in the third; and then the visual mode is again stressed in a more personal way in paragraph four. A varied sensory experience is created:

> When we came to this court today, on this *beautiful springtime morning*, the *profusion of flowers* was *radiant* and *breathtaking*. Each *bloom* seemed to be vying with its neighbor, and altogether they almost outdid themselves. What a *sight* to gladden our hearts, sooth our spirits: Longfellow spoke of the *flowers* thus: "*Stars* of the earth, these *golden flowers; emblems* of the *bright* and *better land*." But the *flowers* and their message of inspiration were for you and me; not for John Demmons. He could not, and did not, *see a flower* as he came to court today. He will never *see a flower* again.
>
> In *happier times*, when John Demmons came home from work, his youngest children met him at the gate of his *humble* rented cottage, and he would *hold them close*, then *throw them into the air* and *catch them* as they came down, *holding them close* so that he *felt their little heartbeats -- flesh of his flesh, blood of his blood, bone of his bone*. For all fathers this *feeling* is about as *great a boon* as God can grant unto you. But now John cannot have the *ecstasy* and *happiness* he formerly knew. He might not be able to *catch the child*, so *he dare not throw it into the air*. How much is the loss of that *privilege worth?*

Go with me now inside the little rented cottage at mealtime. Seven people sit around a table: the father, the mother, and five little children. Before the meal begins, each one clasps the hand of another and forms a family circle. John *tells* one of them to *say grace*, to *"ask the blessing."* And he carefully *listens* to the child as he prays: "God is great, God is good…"

John used to *peek to see* if all the children had closed *their eyes* -- a father's privilege. He cannot *peek* now; he cannot see them. The meal is eaten, but somehow things have changed, and it will never be as it once was.[134]

## ANALOGY

One technique for making language vivid is the use of *analogy*. Nothing allegedly moves jurors more convincingly than an apt comparison to something they know to be true from their own personal experience.[135] For instance, a lawyer for a plaintiff burned in a nuclear power plant accident might liken the facility to a volcano erupting out of control. Or counsel might refer to a chameleon that changes color when it gets frightened as an analogy to describe the other side when it changes its story.

Analogies are vivid and persuasive because they provoke and then reward your audience's intellect and emotions.[136] Having knowledge about erupting volcanoes or chameleons, the judge or jury can then reach their conclusion before the speaker does. Analogies have intense persuasive impact if they are aptly chosen, filled with detail, and never abandoned.[137] As long as they do not violate the "golden rule" by requesting that the jury put themselves in the shoes of one of the parties, analogies are one of the most powerful forms of argument we know.[138]

## METAPHOR

Similar to the analogy is *the metaphor,* another persuasive linguistic tool. A metaphor is a referent that takes a term out of its habitual association and places it in another, more emotional, association. For example, "abortion is legalized *murder*" is a death metaphor. "Allowing this water polluter to freely pollute means the *rape* of our environment" is a sexual assault metaphor. After experimenting with discourse both with and without metaphors, one linguistic researcher concluded that a metaphor *nearly always* communicates a stronger attitude than does a conventional expression.[139]

## RECOMMENDATIONS FOR THE USE OF EMOTIONAL APPEALS

*Note*: Emotionalism in the form of dramatic presentations, visual aids, psychological appeals, and vivid language use are advised for the summation *when they are used in moderation.* Since the jury is already informed about the case, and since the judge will ask them to look at the "facts," the effect of emotion may be expected to be less than in a different sort of persuasive setting.[140] Nevertheless, *some* emotionalism should be used during your closing arguments.

- Make dramatic presentations only when they feel natural for you
- Use visual aids during your summation
- Aim certain appropriate psychological appeals (e.g., justice, pride, love of family) directly at the attitudes and values of your audience
- Use vivid language in order to persuade
- Develop clear and convincing analogies and metaphors

## THE CLOSING ARGUMENT: PRESENTATION

Many of the critical meanings generated in human encounters are elicited by language choice, glance, vocal nuance, gesture, or facial expressions.[141] In other words, we get meaning from linguistic and nonverbal cues. Misunderstanding can come from a listener's insensitivity to these cues, or a speaker's failure to use language and nonverbal cues congruent with the message being communicated to an audience.

For example, if your words express sympathy in the summation, while your voice and face suggest indifference, the jury is likely to believe you to be indifferent rather than sympathetic. Language and delivery influence intelligibility and comprehension. Indeed, they supplement content to a significant degree. Let's examine in greater detail some of the linguistic, vocal, and physical techniques you can use to make your final presentations more effective.

### LANGUAGE AND STYLE

Three familiar qualities of style should always be kept in mind: clarity, intensity, and appropriateness.[142]

#### CLARITY

Perspicuity, or *clarity*, is generally desirable. But "clarity to whom?" is the question. In closing arguments, clarity to judge and jury is the test. Clarity and simplicity are interrelated. Simplicity can come from the use of everyday language. Phrases such as "Isn't that hard to swallow?" or "The bottom dropped out of his case" incorporate slang and clichés. If not overused, they may also provide a great deal of clarity.

The level of difficulty of vocabulary, length of sentences, repetition of key ideas, and transitions are all factors that influence clarity. Terse expressions are usually clearer than longer, overlapping ones. Moderate repetition of key information helps judges and jurors remember. Some redundancy is better than a telegram-like style; it reminds and reinforces.[143] Smooth transitions from one idea to the next also help your listeners follow the flow of your message.

## INTENSITY

As a quality of style, *intensity* refers to the degree to which the language used deviates from neutrality.[144] Speakers using this stylistic quality appear dynamic or energetic.[145] In turn, dynamism enhances their credibility. For instance, the word *must* is more intense than the diluted word *hope*. *Ran out of the building* has more action and intensity than *departed the building*. Employing imagery to describe the case story vividly also provides intensity. Finally, the plaintiff's attorney should use the active voice for intensity, while defense counsel should use the passive voice.[146] Action verbs in the active voice (such as *slapped him*) are more intense than when used in the passive voice (*was slapped*). Language intensity (i.e., powerful language) is especially important for prosecutors and plaintiff's attorneys to use.[147]

Be aware, however, that caution is required regarding intensity. If a listener perceives too many intensifying adjectives (for example, "*very* clear," "*surely* appreciate," and "*definitely* help"), the result is not convincing.[148] A "boomerang effect" from the exaggeration is created, which leads to attitude change in a direction opposite to the one desired.[149] Men are generally more effective than women when using highly intense language.[150] Perhaps stereotypically we *expect* women to use less intense language than men. "When a female communicator uses highly intense language, there may be a violation of expectations for an audience member, which could lead to the rejection of the source and her message."[151] Right or wrong, culturally induced stereotypes and their effects must be taken into account in persuasive communication.

## APPROPRIATENESS

*Appropriateness* of language is essentially a matter of subjective judgment, but the choices you make regarding use of language will suggest to your audience your taste, sensitivity, education, and social attitudes.

Language must be adapted to the audience. You must avoid the use of the word "I," which is egotistical and makes what you are saying sound like a personal belief, and it is an approach forbidden by the American Bar Association.[152] You should also avoid *my client,* which sounds impersonal or like a cashbox ringing,[153] and *deliberately lying,* which is difficult for jurors to accept. Equally inappropriate are certain worthless toss-away phrases, such as:

> *We are here today...*
> *It must be remembered that...*
> *It must be noted that...*
> *I would submit that...*
> *I would contend that...*
> *If I should misstate the evidence, follow your own recollection and not mine.*[154]

Are quotations and anecdotes appropriate? Sometimes. Some lawyers often quote the Bible or Shakespeare. Other lawyers tell anecdotal stores that will occasionally contain dashes of humor. Excessive quotations, stories that counter your overall presentational style, or material that does not fit the facts of your case make your argument seem "contrived or even evasive [and] ... may create the wrong impression."[155]

Some words, because of their connotations, are more appropriate for one side of a case than for the other side. For example, in one highly publicized war-of-words trial in which an obstetrician-gynecologist was convicted of manslaughter in connection with a late abortion, the terms used to characterize the object of the abortion were appropriately *baby* and *child* for the prosecution, and *fetus* or *product of conception* for the defense.[156] In civil suits, as another example, the plaintiff's attorney should use the term *collision*; the defense attorney should refer to it as an *accident*.

Taken together, clarity, intensity, and appropriateness all add to a powerful attorney style. Research findings support the claim that such style is directly related to judge and jury assessments of your competence in the courtroom.[157] It behooves every attorney to be aware of the importance of the linguistic dimensions of closing arguments.

## VOCAL DELIVERY

Your closing argument should be presented in a friendly, conversational, and direct manner.[158] The jury should be talked *with*, not at. Oratory will not do the job. After all, research shows that if you are calm and measured in your vocal delivery, you will be more credible than if your voice is strident and intense.[159]

The presentation of the summation should neither be too loud nor too soft. Nor should it be too fast or too slow. Too much volume and speed implies slipperiness and shallowness.[160] Yet slow, soft talkers are uninteresting and less persuasive.[161] Vocal variety should replace monotony in order to keep the judge and jury interested in your message. Your voice can be raised or lowered when an important point is reached, as long as you do not allow your pitch to become too harsh. Extremely high-pitched voices are less credible than voices with deeper pitches.[162] Think for a moment of the voice pitch of well-known news broadcasters.

Pauses can be used to create suspense and drama; they are particularly useful before and after making main points. Pausing is the equivalent of punctuation in writing and is inappropriate in the middle of an idea or when used every few words. Vocalized pauses (such as *uh* or *um*) between sentences and thoughts should be avoided. Their appearance in speech causes significantly lower listener ratings on speaker credibility, dynamism, and competence.[163] Finally, your closing argument should neither be memorized nor read verbatim. Canned speeches sound insincere and are unimpressive.

## PHYSICAL DELIVERY

Physical delivery involves the message carried by your face, eyes, gestures, whole body movement, and use of space. The prime point to grasp about nonverbal communication is *how to keep from sending the wrong message with it.* Your facial expression, for instance, must be suitable to the information being conveyed during delivery of your closing argument. Inadvertent grimaces and grins distract from a serious appeal to the judge or jury. You should be aware of your typical facial patterns when speaking. Videotaping or getting feedback from observers helps. Eye contact should not be at the floor or some spot about the audience's heads. Such ineffective eye contact rightly or wrongly communicates that "you might feel guilty about something, are shy, or possibly do not like us very much."[164] Rather, direct eye contact should be established with the judge or jurors as the summation is being delivered. Effective eye contact usually enhances sincerity and honesty; it also allows for feedback. In order to ensure maximum eye contact, minimal notes should be used. Reading aloud should be restricted to quoting from the record.

Gestures should be natural, yet not so frequent as to make you appear like a perpetual windmill. You should not be locked physically to one spot unless the court requires you to remain behind a lectern. Even then, you must not anchor yourself to the lectern. If movement is allowed, you should move at key moments in your message in order to gain attention. You should not, however, pace nervously back and forth.

Space is also important. Space is related to your personal height and weight. As we have mentioned, larger (and louder) attorneys may want to be as much as 20 feet away from the jury when speaking. Attorneys smaller in stature who speak in a conversational style may want to be as close as 4 or 5 feet away. One study indicates that distances between the speaker and listener of more than 12 feet are the most effective for one-way persuasion.[165]

In order to gain physical presence with your jury or judge, stand directly in front of them so they pay close attention. Move as you go from argument to argument, but do not pace. Constant pacing is distracting to an audience and makes you appear nervous.[166] At the same time, do not intimidate your jury by hollering, speaking loudly, pounding on the jury rail, and "getting into the face of the jury." This may look good on television, but such behavior does not win lawsuits."[167]

How can you develop an effective vocal and physical delivery? The answer is not to think of what you are doing during the actual performance of your closing argument; "an awareness ... destroys naturalness and spontaneity... [it] results in selfconsciousness."[168] The road to an improved delivery is found instead in being prepared, feeling comfortable, practicing aloud, and performing often.

## RECOMMENDATIONS FOR PRESENTING THE CLOSING ARGUMENT

- Use clear language, short sentences, repetition, and smooth transitions
- Use intense language, especially if you are a male
- Use appropriate language by adapting to the taste, sensitivity, education, and social attitudes of your audience
- Speak in a conversational tone
- Vary your volume, speed, and pitch
- Use pauses effectively and avoid vocalized pauses such as "um" and "uh"
- Maintain eye contact with your audience; use minimal notes
- Use natural gestures and movement

## THE CLOSING ARGUMENT: PREPARATION

Preparation of the closing argument involves careful planning, ongoing note-taking, pre-delivery outlining, audience analysis, and rehearsal. Closing arguments are sometimes given immediately after the last witness has testified or after a short or overnight recess. Since you usually do not know how much preparation time you will have for giving the closing argument, *careful planning* must occur throughout the course of the trial. After all, "very few lawyers can make an effective impromptu argument."[169] The best final argument is one that has been carefully planned and prepared.[170]

Preparation for the closing argument is an ongoing process. In fact, preparation of both the opening statement and the closing argument should occur simultaneously so that the two speeches integrate smoothly. The main difference between the two speeches is that in the former, you can only preview the facts, and in the latter, you can argue desired inferences from the facts. Therefore, there is an added need for preparation of the closing argument.

Before and during the trial, you should jot down items that might be included in your summation. One item you should review is the set of notes that you took during your opponent's opening statement. As noted earlier, you want to see if your opponents proved what they claimed they would prove. These items can be kept on tear sheets in a trial notebook. When individual items or ideas are kept to a single sheet, the material can easily be indexed for ready reference throughout the trial and then rearranged as needed.

At or near the end of a trial, you should sort through the tear sheets and assemble them into a cogent *outline*. Your speech should never be written out verbatim. Like an architect designing a home who has a clear picture of the building before proceeding with the details, you must know the major ideas to be covered and images to be formed. Your outline should be organized so as to summarize the case theory for the court in a logical and dramatic way. That means being consistent with what was said throughout the opening statement and the witnesses' testimony. Without a well-designed plan for summation, you will frequently fail to recognize the most efficacious point at which your speech should be terminated.[171]

As you prepare your closing remarks, you need to engage in *audience analysis,* that is, to think about how to adapt to the particular judge or jury in the case. Often statements made by jurors during voir dire may provide a valuable clue to points that should be emphasized in summation.[172] As stressed earlier in this book, jury decisions are not made on rational arguments and case facts alone, but also on emotions, feelings, prejudices, and values.

Along these lines, consider the following scenario: Assume you are a plaintiff's attorney trying to convince a jury in a personal injury case that the plaintiff's mental health was damaged. You recognize the problem is invisible to the jury. Therefore, in closing argument, you must deal directly with the problem of a jury disinclined to accept hidden and subjective symptoms of suffering. But how can you arouse in the jury a sense of identification with the plaintiff? You must find exciting language and analogies to make the mental anguish as vivid as possible. (Recall the linguistic techniques discussed earlier.) You might also play upon the lawyer-client-juror value similarities relevant to this attempt to persuade.[173] (Recall the anchoring technique.)

Finally, I would strongly advise that you *rehearse* your closing argument. *Practicing aloud* can provide some notion of how your summation will sound. If possible, a tape recorder, video camera, and/or a listener to give feedback to the practical argument is helpful. "A review of the presentation ... will usually lead to a change in delivery. Even experienced trial attorneys discover they must make adjustments."[174]

# AFTERWORD

This book has been written from a trial consultant's perspective to assist you in becoming a more persuasive advocate in court, especially in the presentation of your opening statements and closing arguments. What appears here represents only the tip of the iceberg in terms of what must be done by you to influence judges and juries. Voir dire and witness examination play equally important roles in the overall process of persuasion.

From time to time, it is advisable to seek help from consultants who can diagnose problems and offer solutions that are unique to your case and your communication needs. Choosing a well-trained and experienced trial consultant who is knowledgeable in persuasion and the litigation process can be an invaluable asset in presenting and arguing your case.

The trial consultant's primary job is not to help you untangle the legal aspects of your case (although some consultants are also attorneys), but rather to help you focus on how to select your jury and then present your case in the most coherent and compelling manner possible. Litigation consultants can also help you with mock trials, focus groups, fact and expert witness preparation, graphics, voir dire questions, jury de-selection (including juror profiles and supplemental juror questionnaires), opening statements and closing arguments, and overall trial strategy.

How can you find a trial consultant who can help you? The answer is to view the membership directory provided at the website of the American Society of Trial Consultants. (www.astcweb.org) The directory, updated annually, is organized alphabetically by member name, geographically by state, and by specialized areas of consulting.

For more information about trial consultants, contact the American Society of Trial Consultants, 1941 Greenspring Drive, Timonium, MD 21093. Telephone (410) 560-7949.

Whether you seek outside help or do it on your own, you are reminded that in court, you must be a master of the spoken word. Effective advocacy means effective communication and persuasion. I trust that this book has helped you to move at least one step closer to being the master advocate you wish to be.

## ABOUT THE AUTHOR

**Ronald J. Matlon**, Ph.D. is CEO and Senior Litigation Consultant with Matlon and Associates, a trial consulting firm based in Maryland. His areas of consulting expertise are in witness preparation, attorney advocacy skills, voir dire questioning, jury selection, and case strategy through the use of focus groups. He appears regularly as a seminar and workshop presenter at bar associations and law firms. Since 1984, he has served as the Executive Director of the American Society of Trial Consultants, of which he was one of the founders and a Past President.

Dr. Matlon is also a former Professor and Chairperson of the Department of Speech and Mass Communication at Towson University. His area of teaching and research was in legal communication, argumentation and advocacy, and rhetoric/persuasion. Dr. Matlon received a B.A. degree from Indiana State University as well as M.S. and Ph.D. degrees from Purdue University. He has authored six books, including Communication in the Legal Process and Communication Strategies in the Practice of Lawyering. Professor Matlon has written articles and made many public presentations, most of them on some aspect of persuasion in the courtroom. His consulting address is 2324 Carroll Mill Road, Phoenix, MD 21131. His website is www.matlonlitigation.com

## REFERENCES


1. J. Jeans, *Trial Advocacy* (St. Paul: West, 1975), 144.
2. C.I. Hovland, "Summary and Implications," in C.I. Hovland et al., eds., *The Order of Presentation in Persuasion* (New Haven: Yale University Press, 1957), 139.
3. F.H. Lund, "The Psychology of Belief: The Law of Primacy in Persuasion," *Journal of Abnormal and Social Psychology,* 20 (1925), 183-191.
4. S.E. Asch, "Forming Impressions of Personality," *Journal of Abnormal and Social Psychology,* 41 (1946), 258-290.
5. A.S. Luchins, "Primacy-Recency in Impression Formation," in C.I. Hovland et al., eds., *The Order of Presentation in Persuasion,* op. cit., 33-61.
6. H.P. Weld and E. R. Danzig, "A Study of the Way in Which a Verdict Is Reached by a Jury," *American Journal of Psychology,* 53 (1940), 518-536.
7. R.T. Marshall, "The Telling Opening Statement," *Practical Lawyer* (October, 1973), 32.
8. V.A. Stone, "A Primacy Effect in Decision-Making by Jurors," *Journal of Communication,* 19 (1969), 239-247.
9. T.A. Pyszczynski and L.S. Wrightsman, "The Effects of Opening Statements on Mock Jurors' Verdicts in a Simulated Criminal Trial," *Journal of Applied Social Psychology,* 11 (1981), 301-313.
10. N.H. Anderson, "Primacy Effects in Personality Impression Formation Using a Generalized Order Effect Paradigm," *Journal of Personality and Social Psychology,* 2 (1965), 1-9.
11. N.H. Anderson and A. Jacobson, "Effect of Stimulus Inconsistency and Discounting Instructions in Personality Impression Formation," *Journal of Personality and Social Psychology,* 2 (1965), 531-539.
12. M.F. Kaplan, "Context Effects in Impression Formation: The Weighted Averaging versus the Meaning-Change Formation," *Journal of Personality and Social Psychology,* 19 (1971), 92-99; R.S. Wyer, Jr. and S. F. Watson, "Context Effects in Impression Formation," *Journal of Personality and Social Psychology,* 12 (1969), 22-33.

13. For an elaboration of these three variables, see R. E. Lana, "Controversy of the Topic and the Order of Presentation of Persuasive Communication," *Psychological Reports* (1963), 163-170; R. E. Lana, "Familiarity and the Order of Presentation of Persuasive Communication," *Journal of Abnormal and Social Psychology,* 62 (1961), 573-577; R. E. Lana, "Interest, Media, and Order Effects in Persuasive Communications," *Journal of Psychology,* 56 (1963), 9-13.
14. R.J. Crawford and C.A. Morris, *The Persuasive Edge* (Tucson: Lawyers and Judges Publishing Company, 2006), 5.
15. H. Cromwell, "The Relative Effect on Audience Attitude of the First versus the Second Argumentative Speech of a Series," *Speech Monographs,* 17 (1950), 105-122.
16. R. G. Lawson, "The Law of Primacy in the Criminal Courtroom," *Journal of Social Psychology,* 77 (1969), 121-131.
17. R. G. Lawson, "Order of Presentation as a Factor in Jury Persuasion," *Kentucky Law Journal,* 56 (1967-68), 523-555.
18. R. J. Crawford, "Opening Statement for the Defense- A Patch of Blue," paper presented to the Speech Communication Association (Anaheim, CA: November, 1981), 2.
19. J. H. Lingle and T. M. Ostrom, "Principles of Memory and Cognition in Attitude Formation," in R. E. Tetty, T. M. Ostrom and T. C. Brock, eds., *Cognitive Responses in Persuasion* (Hillsdale, NJ: Erlhaum, 1981), 401.
20. R. C. Anderson and J. W. Pickert, "Recall of Previously Unreadable Information Following a Shift in Perspective," *Journal of Verbal Learning and Verbal Behavior,* 17 (1978), 1-12; G. H. Bower, J. B. Black, and T. J. Turner, "Scripts in Comprehension and Memory," *Cognitive Psychology,* 11 (1979), 177-220.
21. D. Linz, S. Penrod, and E. McDonald, "Attorney Communication and Impression Making in the Courtroom," *Law and Human Behavior,* 10 (1986), 283.
22. G. H. Bower, "Cognitive Psychology: An Introduction, in W. K. Estes, ed., *Handbook of Learning and Cognitive Processes,* Volume I (Hillside, NJ: Erlbaum, 1975), 25-80.

23. P. W. Thorndyke, "Cognitive Structures in Comprehension and Memory of Narrative Discourse," *Cognitive Psychology*, 9 (1977), 77-110.
24. Pyszczynski and Wrightsman, op. cit.
25. K. Broda-Bahm, "Getting Beyond the Catchy Phrase and Creating a Trial Theme that Truly Works," *The Jury Expert* (July, 2008), 1-8.
26. Jeans, op. cit., 200-201.
27. L. Decof, *Art of Advocacy: Opening Statement* (New York: Matthew Bender, 1982), 0 1-40 – 1-42
28. R. C. McFigg et al., *Civil Trial Manual* (Los Angeles: Joint Committee on Legal Education of the American Law Institute and the American Bar Association, 1974), 395.
29. G. A. LaMarca, "Opening Statements- Effective Techniques," in J. J. Kennelly, ed., *Trial Lawyer's Guide: 1977 Annual* (Wilmette, IL: Callaghan and Company, 1977), 447.
30. J. A. Call, "The Trial as Story," *Trial* (November, 1986), 84.
31. W. L. Bennett and M. S. Feldman, *Restructuring Reality in the Courtroom* (New Brunswick, NJ: Rutgers University Press, 1981), 3.
32. Ibid., 5.
33. A. J. Cone and V. Lawyer, "The Act of Persuasion in Litigation," (Des Moines: Dean- Hicks, 1966), 268.
34. Ibid., 269.
35. D. Ball, "Damages: The Basics," *The Jury Expert* (June 2005), 1-7.
36. E. Cooper and H. Dinerman, "Analysis of the Film, 'Don't Be a Sucker': A Study in Communication," *Public Opinion Quarterly*, 15 (1951), 243-264; B. J. Fine, "Conclusion-Drawing, Communicator Credibility, and Anxiety as Factors in Opinion Change," *Journal of Abnormal and Social Psychology*, 54 (1957), 369-374; C. I. Hovland and W. Mandell, "An Experimental Comparison of Conclusion-Drawing by the Communicator and Audience," *Journal of Abnormal and Social Psychology*, 47 (1952), 582-588; N. R. F. Maier and R. A. Maier, "An Experimental Test

of the Effects of 'Developmental' versus 'Free' Discussion on the Quality of Group Decision," *Journal of Applied Psychology*, 41 (1957), 320-323

37. W. H. Mitchell, "Voir Dire and Opening Statement/The Defense Takes the Offense," *Federation of Insurance Counsel Quarterly*, 26 (1976), 141.
38. J. D. Fuchsberg, "Opening Statements- Plaintiff's View," in American Jurisprudence, *Trials*, Volume 5 (San Francisco: Bancroft-Whitney, 1966), 296.
39. W. J. McGuire, "Inducing Resistance to Persuasion," in L. Berkowitz, ed., *Advances in Experimental Psychology*, Volume I (New York: Academic Press, 1964), 192-231.
40. W. J. McGuire and D. Papageorgis, "Effectiveness of Forewarning in Developing Resistance to Persuasion," *Public Opinion Quarterly*, 26 (1962), 24-34.
41. R. E. Petty and J. T. Cacioppo, "Forewarning, Cognitive Responding, and Resistance to Persuasion," *Journal of Personality and Social Psychology*, 35 (1977), 645-655. This study was updated and confirmed by the same authors in "Effects of Forewarning and Persuasive Intent and Involvement on Cognitive Responses and Persuasion," *Personality and Social Psychology Bulletin*, 5 (1979), 173-176.
42. A. A. Lumsdaine and I. L. Janis, "Resistance to 'Counterpropoganda' Produced by One-Sided and Two-Sided 'Propaganda' Presentations," *Public Opinion Quarterly*, 17 (1953), 311-318
43. Litigation Sciences, "Affective and Cognitive Jurors," *Trial*, 18 (1982), 95.
44. T. A. Pyszczynski, J. Greenberg, D. Mack, and L. S. Wrightsman, "Opening Statements in a Jury Trial: The Effect of Promising More than the Evidence Can Show," *Journal of Applied Social Psychology*, 11 (1981), 434-444.
45. F. X. Busch, *Trial Procedure Materials* (Indianapolis: Bobbs-Merrill, 1961), 137.
46. R. M. Markus, "A Theory of Trial Advocacy," *Tulane Law Review*, 56 (1981), 119.

47. T. A. Mauet, *Fundamentals of Trial Techniques* (Boston: Little, Brown, 1980), 51.
48. J. C. Elam, "Persuasion in the Opening Statement: The Defendant's Approach," in G. W. Holmes, ed., *Persuasion: The Key to Damages* (Ann Arbor: MI: The Institute of Continuing Legal Education, 1978), 97.
49. R. W. Buchanan, "Opening Statements and Closing Arguments: A Response from the Communication Perspective," in R. J. Matlon and R. J. Crawford, eds., *Proceedings of the 1983 Conference on Communication Strategies in the Practice of Lawyering* (Annandale, VA: Speech Communication Association, 1983), 454.
50. Crawford, note 18, p.11.
51. W. L. Bennett, "Storytelling in Criminal Trials: A Model of Social Judgment," *Quarterly Journal of Speech*, 64 (1968), 1-22; Bennett and Feldman, note 31, Chapter 3.
52. Crawford, op. cit., 10-11.
53. M. G. Parkinson, "Verbal Behavior and Courtroom Success," *Communication Education*, 30 (1981), 22-31.
54. "Proximate What? Only a Ph. D. Knew," *American Bar Association Journal*, 64 (1978), 660.
55. D.F. Wyzga, "A Communication Strategy: The Importance of Place in Your Legal Story," *The Jury Expert* (February, 2007), 12.
56. D. Peters, "Participatory Persuasion: Strategies and Research Needs in Opening Statements and Closing Arguments," in Matlon and Crawford, note 49, pp. 403-404.
57. L. Nizer, *My Life in Court* (Garden City: NY Doubleday, 1961), 137-138.
58. C. Spangenberg, "Basic Values and the Techniques of Persuasion," *Litigation*, 3 (1977), 16.
59. D. S. Gouran, "Principles Affecting the Choice of Persuasive Strategies in Opening and Closing Arguments," in K. P. Taylor, ed., *Trial Advocacy: Strategic Considerations in Persuasion* (Orlando, FL: Institute for Study of the Trial, 1980), 22.
60. T. Riley, "The Opening Statement: Winning at the Outset," *American Journal of Trial Advocacy*, 3 (1979), 233-234.
61. C. I. Hovland, I. L. Janis, and H. H. Kelley, *Communication and Persuasion* (New Haven: Yale University Press, 1953), 290.

62. P. G. Zimbardo and F. L. Ruch, *Psychology and Life* (Glenview, IL: Scott Foresman, 1975), 232-273.
63. Adapted from D. Ehninger, B. E. Gronbeck, R. E. McKerrow, and A. H. Monroe, *Principles and Types of Speech Communication* (Glenview, IL: Scott Foresman, 1982), 151-156.
64. R. J. Klienman, "Opening Statements," *Trial* (September, 1987), 43.
65. S. Chaiken and A. H. Eagly, "Communication Modality as a Determinant of Message Persuasiveness and Message Comprehension," *Journal of Personality and Social Psychology,* 34 (1976), 605-614.
66. J.S. Bell, "Using Visuals to Reinforce Theme," *The Jury Expert* (September, 2003) 10.
67. T. Sannito, "The Role of the Forensic Psychologist in the Courtroom Drama," *Trial Diplomacy Journal* (Fall, 1987), 11.
68. Decof, note 27, pp. 1-37; R. M. Herman, "Using the Opening Statement to Maximum Advantage," in *How to Relate to, Communicate with, and Influence Juries* (Baltimore: Trial Lawyers' Association, 1987), 19.
69. V.H. Starr, "From the Communication Professor: Communication Strategies and Research Needs on Opening Statements and Closing Arguments," in Matlon and Crawford, op. cit., 440.
70. E. A. Hess, "Attitude and Pupil Size," *Scientific American,* 212 (1965), 46-54.
71. K. Friedman, "Learning the Arabs' Silent Language: Edward J. Hall Interviewed," *Psychology Today,* (1979), 46-47.
72. M. Cooper, "The Impressive Voice in the Courtroom," *Trial,* 15 (1979), 53.
73. M. W. Littleton, "Opening to the Court or Jury," in H. Bodin, ed., *Civil Litigation and Trial Techniques* (New York: Practicing Law Institute, 1976), 310.
74. Elam, op. cit., 97.
75. R. J. Matlon, J. W. Davis, B. Catchings, W. Derr, and V. Waldron, "Factors Affecting Jury Decision-Making," a paper presented to the Speech Communication Association (Denver: November, 1985); B. J. Tarter-Hilgendorf, "Impact of Opening and Closing Statements," *Trial* (November, 1986), 70-80.

76. M. Sams, Jr., "Closing Argument: New Answers to Some Old Problems," in G. W. Holmes, ed., *Excellence in Advocacy* (Ann Arbor, MI: Institute of Continuing Legal Education, 1971), 86.
77. J. A. Seckinger and K. S. Broun, Problems and Cases in *Trial Advocacy* (St. Paul: National Institute for Legal Advocacy, 1979), 186.
78. Ibid., 74.
79. Weld and Danzig, note 6, p. 531.
80. L. H. Vogel, "Final Argument," in Bodin, op. cit., 646.
81. S. Zdep and W. Wilson, "Recency Effects in Opinion Formation," *Psychological Reports*, 23 (1968), 195-200.
82. C. A. Insko, "Primary versus Recency as a Function of the Timing of Arguments and Measures," *Journal of Abnormal and Social Psychology*, 69 (1964), 381-391; C. A. Insko, E. A. Lind, and S. LaTour, "Persuasion, Recall and Thoughts," *Representative Research in Social Psychology*, 7 (1976), 66-78; N. Miller and D. T. Campbell, "Recency and Primacy in Persuasion as a Function of the Timing of Speech and Measurements," *Journal of Abnormal and Social Psychology*, 59 (1959), 1-9.
83. L. Walker, J. Thibault, and V. Andreoli, "Order of Presentation at Trial," *Yale Law Journal*, 82 (1972), 216-226; W. Wallace and W. Wilson, "Reliable Recency Effects," *Psychology Reports*, 25 (1969), 311-317.
84. Starr, op. cit., 437.
85. S. M. Speiser, "Closing Argument," *The Docket* (Fall, 1986), 1.
86. Buchanan, note 49, p. 453.
87. J. W. McElhaney, "Solving Problems with Final Argument," *Litigation* (Winter, 1983), 43.
88. Vogel, op. cit., 646.
89. P. H. Marshall, "Persuading Judges in Bench Trials," *Litigation* (Summer, 1977), 12.
90. M. L. Gordon, "Nonjury Summations," in American Jurisprudence, *Trials*, Volume 6 (San Francisco: Bancroft-Whitney, 1967), 776-777.
91. G. E. Mills, Unpublished and undated information on legal argument, 209-210.

92. Busch, note 45, pp. 526-527.
93. H. A. Kuvin, *Trial Handbook* (Englewood Cliffs, NJ: Prentice-Hall, 1965), 283.
94. E. J. Thompson, "Lawyers' Courtroom Conduct and Manners," *Case and Comment* (September-October, 1967), 22.
95. J. A. Tanford, *The Trial Process: Law, Tactics, and Ethics* (Charlottesville, VA: Michie, 1983), 142.
96. Dunlop v. United States, 165 U.S. 486, S. Ct. 374, 41 L. Ed. 789 (1987)
97. J. J. Makay and T. C. Sawyer, *Speech Communication Now: An Introduction to Rhetorical Influences* (Columbus, OH: Merrill, 1973), 142.
98. N. E. Fontes and R. W. Bundens, "Persuasion During the Trial Process," in M. E. Roloff and G. R. Miller, eds., *Persuasion: New Directions in Theory and Research* (Beverly Hills, CA: Sage, 1980), 249-266.
99. Crawford and Morris, op. cit., 196.
100. L.J. Smith, *Art of Advocacy: Summation* (New York: Matthew Bender, 1981), 1-17.
101. Tanford, op. cit., 156.
102. B. J. Calder, C. A. Insko, and B. Yandell, "The Relation of Cognitive and Memorial Process to Persuasion in a Simulated Jury Trial," *Journal of Applied Social Psychology*, 4 (1974), 62-93.
103. Smith, op. cit., 1-34.
104. J. D. Lee, "Final Strokes: Painting the Whole Picture at Summation," *Trial* (July, 1982), 66.
105. D. Cohen, "Reasonable Doubt in Summation," *Trial Diplomacy Journal* (Spring, 1981), 32.
106. D. Hirschberg and G. Isaac, *Advanced Criminal Tactics* (New York: Practicing Law Institute, 1978), 204-205; McFigg, et al., note 28, p. 453.
107. P. Bergman, *Trial Advocacy* (St. Paul, West, 1979), 252.
108. Hovland and Mandell, note 36; D. L. Thistlewaite, H. DeHaan, and J. Kamenetzky, "The Effects of 'Directive' and 'Nondirective' Communication Procedures on Attitudes," *Journal of Abnormal and Social Psychology*, 51 (1955), 107-113.

109. D. E. Vinson and P. K. Anthony, "The Closing Argument: Applications of Attribution Theory," *Trial Diplomacy Journal* (Spring, 1984), 34.
110. R. A. Jones and J. W. Brehm, "Persuasiveness of One-and Two-Sided Communications as a Function of Awareness That There Are Two Sides," *Journal of Experimental Social Psychology,* 6 (1970), 47-56.
111. S. H. Goldberg, *The First Trial: Where Do I Sit? What Do I Say?* (St. Paul; West, 1982), 204-205.
112. Bergman, op. cit., 321.
113. M.F. Colley, "Friendly Persuasion: Gaining Attention, Comprehension and Acceptance in Court," *Trial* (August, 1981), 46.
114. Mauet, note 47, p. 301.
115. J. P. Miller, "Opening and Closing Statements from the Viewpoint of the Plaintiff's Attorney," *Practical Lawyer* (October, 1964), 92.
116. Berman, op. cit., 311-318.
117. P. R. Biddle, "An Experimental Study of Ethos and Appeal for Overt Behavior in Persuasion," unpublished Ph. D. dissertation (University of Illinois, 1966); H. Leventhal and R. P. Singer, "Affect Arousal and Positioning of Recommendations in Persuasive Communications," *Journal of Personality and Social Psychology,* 4 (1966), 137-146.
118. M. M. Belli, "Techniques of Final Argument," *Trial Diplomacy Journal* (Winter, 1979), 39.
119. S. Baldwin, "Jury Argument," *Trial* (April, 1984), 59.
120. S. E. Preiser, "The Criminal Case: Tips on Summation," *Trial* (October, 1979), 53.
121. Spangenberg, note 58, p. 16.
122. R.J. Mongeluzo, "You Only Get One Chance to Make a Great First Impression," *The Jury Expert* (May, 2005) 2.
123. Cone and Lawyer, note 33, p. 335.
124. A. E. Morrill, *Trial Diplomacy* (Chicago: Court Practice Institute, 1979), 95.
125. Tanford, op. cit., 156.
126. Peters, note 56, p. 406.

127. W. J. McGuire, "Cognitive Consistency and Attitude Change," *Journal of Abnormal and Social Psychology*, 60 (1960), 345-353.
128. S. W. Littlejohn, *Theories of Human Communication* (Belmont, CA: Wadsworth, 1989), 88.
129. K. P. Taylor, R. W. Buchanan, and D. W. Strawn, *Communication Strategies for Trial Attorneys* (Glenview, Ill. : Scott Foresman, 1984), 83.
130. Mills, op. cit., 205-207.
131. J. M. Conley, "Language in the Courtroom," *Trial* (September, 1979), 35.
132. E. E. Baker, "The Immediate Effects of Perceived Speaker Disorganization on Change in Perceived Speaker," *Western Speech*, 29 (1965), 148-161; H. Giles and P. F. Powesland, *Speech Styles and Special Evaluating* (New York: Academic Press, 1975); L. S. Harms, "Social Judgement of Status Cues in Language," unpublished Ph. D. dissertation (Ohio State University, 1959); G. R. Miller and M. A. Hewgill, "The Effects of Variations in Nonfluency on Audience Ratings of Source Credibility," *Quarterly Journal of Speech*, 50 (1964), 36-44; A. Mulac, "Assessment and Application of the Revised Speech Dialect Attitudinal Scale," *Communication Monographs*, 43 (1976), 238-245; P. I. Rosenthal, "Specificity, Verifiability, and Message Credibility," *Quarterly Journal of Speech*, 57 (1971), 393-401; K. K. Sereno and G. J. Hawkins, "The Effects of Variations in Speaker's Nonfluency upon Audience Ratings and Attitudes toward the Speech Topic and the Speaker's Credibility," *Speech Monographs*, 34 (1967), 58-64.
133. S. L. Swanson and D. Wenner, "Sensory Language in the Courtroom," *Trial Diplomacy Journal* (Winter, 1981-1982), 14.
134. Judge R. Evans, Jr., Opening and Closing Arguments: The Law in Georgia (Norcross, GA: Harrison, 1978), 42-48.
135. Spangenberg, note 58, 13, 16.
136. Peters, note 56, 404.
137. R. J. Crawford, "Closing Arguments: High Noon at the Penthouse Corral," *Trial Diplomacy Journal* (Winter, 1982-1983), 15.
138. J. W. McElhaney, "Analogy in Final Argument," *Litigation* (Winter, 1980), 37.

139. J. W. Bowers, "Some Correlates of Language Intensity," *Quarterly Journal of Speech*, 50 (1964), 415-420.
140. P. C. Lewan and E. Stotland, "The Effects of Prior Information on Susceptibility to an Emotional Appeal," *Journal of Abnormal and Social Psychology*, 62 (1961), 450-453.
141. D. Barnlund, *Interpersonal Communication* (Boston: Houghton Mifflin, 1968) 535-536.
142. Mills, op. cit., 205-207.
143. J. T. Cacioppo and R. E. Petty, "Effects of Extent of Thought on the Pleasantness Rating of P.O.X. Triads: Evidence of Three Judgmental Tendencies in Evaluating Social Situations," *Journal of Personality and Social Psychology*, 9 (1968), 184-188.
144. J. W. Bowers, "Language Intensity, Social Introversion and Attitude Change," *Speech Monographs*, 30 (2982), 345.
145. W. J. McEwen and B. S. Greenberg, "The Effects of Message Intensity on Receiver Evaluations of Source, Message, and Topic," *Journal of Communication*, 20 (1970), 340-350.
146. M. G. Parkinson, "Two Studies of the Relationship Between Presentation Style and Verdict," Unpublished paper, 1982. Contact: Michael Parkinson, Attorney-at-Law, Parkinson & Parkinson, 501 N. Main Street, Tinckneyville, IL 62274.
147. Parkinson, note 50, p. 29.
148. M. R. Abbey and W. M. O'Barr, "Law and Language: The Duke University Studies," *Trial Diplomacy Journal* (Winter, 1981), 26; J. M. Connely, W. M. O'Barr, and E. A. Lind, "The Power of Language: Presentational Style in the Courtroom," *Duke Law Journal* (January, 1978), 1375.
149. Bowers, "Language Intensity..." op. cit.
150. M. Burgoon and D. Stewart, "Empirical Investigations of Language Intensity: The Effects of Sex of Source, Receiver, and Language Intensity on Attitude Change," *Human Communication Research*, 1 (1975), 244-248.
151. E. P. Bettinghaus, *Persuasive Communication* (New York: Holt, Rinehart & Winston, 1980), 127.
152. Code of Professional Responsibility, DR7-106 (1971).

153. J. W. McElhaney, "The Right Word," *Litigation* (Spring, 1981), 44.
154. J. W. McElhaney, "The Stock Phrases," *Litigation* (Summer, 1982), 44.
155. Speiser, note 85, pp. 7-8.
156. B. Danet, "'Baby' or 'Fetus'?: Language and the Construction of Reality in a Manslaughter Trial," *Semiotica*, 32 (1980), 187-219.
157. H. B. Rothblatt, *Successful Techniques in the Trial of Criminal Cases* (Englewood Cliffs, NJ: Prentice-Hall, 1961), 95.
158. Ibid.
159. J. MacLachlan, "What People Really Think of Fast Talkers," *Psychology Today* (November, 1979), 112-117.
160. N. Miller, G. Maruyama, R. J. Beaber, and K. Valone, "Speed of Speech and Persuasion," *Journal of Personality and Social Psychology* (November, 1979), 112-117.
161. Ibid.
162. D. W. Addington, "The Effect of Vocal Variations on Ratings of Source Credibility," *Speech Monographs*, 38 (1971), 242-247.
163. Miller and Hewgill, note 132.
164. P. K. Anthony and D. E. Vinson, "Nonverbal Communication in the Courtroom," *Trial Diplomacy Journal* (Spring, 1987), 36.
165. S. Albert and J. M. Dabbs, Jr., "Physical Distance and Persuasion," *Journal of Personality and Social Psychology*, 15 (1970), 265-270.
166. Crawford and Morris, op. cit., 39.
167. Lee, note 104, p. 70.
168. J. Stefano, "Body Language and Persuasion," *Litigation* (Summer, 1977).
169. J. Kelner and F. E. McGovern, *Successful Litigation Techniques* (New York: Matthew Bender, 1981), 17-3.
170. F. J. McGarr, "Prosecution Summations," in American Jurisprudence, *Trials*, Volume 6 (San Francisco: Bancroft-Whitney, 1967), 878.
171. H. A. Gair, "Summations for the Plaintiff," in American Jurisprudence, *Trials*, Volume 6 (San Francisco: Bancroft-Whitney, 1967), 651.

172. McFigg, op. cit., 446.
173. E. Berscheid, "Opinion Change and Communicator-Communicatee Similarity and Dissimilarity," *Journal of Personality and Social Psychology*, 4 (1966), 670-680.
174. J. J. Cleary, "The Final Argument in a Criminal Case," *Practical Lawyer* (September, 1981), 45.

# INDEX